W9-CLD-950

INTERNATIONAL ECONOMICS

THE CAMBRIDGE ECONOMIC HANDBOOKS

General Editors

J. M. KEYNES (Lord Keynes)	1922–1936
D. H. ROBERTSON (Sir Dennis Robertson)	1936–1946
C. W. GUILLEBAUD	1946–1956
C. W. GUILLEBAUD ⎱ **MILTON FRIEDMAN** ⎰	1956–

INTERNATIONAL ECONOMICS

BY

SIR ROY HARROD

Student of Christ Church, Oxford

DIGSWELL PLACE

JAMES NISBET & CO. LTD.

CAMBRIDGE

AT THE UNIVERSITY PRESS

First published . . . . *May 1933*

Revised and Reset . . *January 1939*

Reprinted . . . . . *February 1942*
1945, 1946, 1947, 1948, 1949, 1951,
1952, 1955, 1956,

Revised and Reset *1957*

Reprinted *1959, 1960*

James Nisbet and Co. Ltd.
and the Cambridge University Press
in association with the University of Chicago Press

INTRODUCTION BY THE GENERAL EDITOR

SHORTLY after the war of 1914–18 there seemed to be a place for a Series of introductory Economic Handbooks "intended to convey to the ordinary reader and to the uninitiated student some conception of the general principles of thought which economists now apply to economic problems."

This Series was planned by the late Lord Keynes under the title *Cambridge Economic Handbooks*, and he wrote for it a general Editorial Introduction of which the words quoted above formed part. In 1936 Lord Keynes handed over the editorship of the Series to Mr. D. H. Robertson, who held it until he became Professor of Economics in the University of London.[1]

The judgment of its originators has been justified by the wide welcome given to the Series. Apart from its circulation in the British Empire, it has been published from the start in the United States of America while translations of the principal volumes have so far appeared in German, Spanish, Italian, Swedish, Japanese, Polish and Lithuanian.

It is symptomatic of the changes which have been taking place in recent times in the development of economic science, changes associated in a high degree with the work and influence of Lord Keynes himself, that within the brief space of fifteen years the text of part of the Editorial Introduction should have stood in need of revision. In its original version the last paragraph of the Introduction to the Series ran as follows:

"Even on matters of principle there is not yet a complete unanimity of opinion amongst professors. Generally speaking, the writers of these volumes believe themselves to be orthodox members of the Cambridge School of Economics. At any rate, most of their ideas about the subject, and even their prejudices, are traceable to the contact they have enjoyed with the writings and lectures of the two economists who have chiefly influenced Cambridge thought for the past fifty years, Dr. Marshall and Professor Pigou."

When the Editorship of the Series was transferred to Mr. Robertson, Lord Keynes consented to the retention of his general Intro-

[1] Professor Robertson now holds the Chair of Political Economy in the University of Cambridge.

duction, but subsequently re-wrote the concluding paragraph in the following form:

"Even on matters of principle there is not yet a complete unanimity of opinion amongst professional students of the subject. Immediately after the war daily economic events were of such a startling character as to divert attention from theoretical complexities. But to-day, economic science has recovered its wind. Traditional treatments and traditional solutions are being questioned, improved, and revised. In the end this activity of research should clear up controversy. But for the moment controversy and doubt are increased. The writers of this series must apologise to the general reader and to the beginner if many parts of their subject have not yet reached to a degree of certainty and lucidity which would make them easy and straightforward reading."

Still more recent events have produced a world so far removed from that which existed when the foregoing words were written, that it has fallen to the lot of the present Editor to provide a new Introduction.

This is perhaps a good vantage point from which to survey very briefly some of the principal trends in the evolution of economic thought in this country during the past thirty years. Prior to 1914 economic theory here was largely dominated by Alfred Marshall; and economists, following him, thought in terms of the long period tendencies of the different sections of the economic system towards postitions of equilibrium, even though ever-present dynamic factors were perpetually modifying the existing structure and presenting new and equally distant, if equally unattainable, goals as stimuli to change and adaptation. Moreover, in the Marshallian system, those tendencies resulted from the working of persistent underlying forces which were conceived of as largely competitive in character. The increasing trend towards monopoly was certainly affecting thought, but not so much in the realm of the theory of value as in the emphasis which came to be laid on possible discrepancies between the private interest and the social interest. Under the influence of Professor Pigou a Welfare Economics was developing side by side with, and out of, the Value Economics of the older generation.

After 1918 the long-drawn-out agony of the depressed areas, the weakening of the position of this country in international trade, and the tremendous intensity of the economic crisis of 1930–32 (to mention but a few out of the many contributing causes) combined, on the one hand, to focus attention on problems of the short period and, on the other hand, to throw doubt on the extent to which the self-adjusting, seemingly automatic mechanism, which on the whole had operated so effectively during the nineteenth century, was capable of coping with the deep-seated maladjustments and disharmonies which characterised the post-war world. At the same time value theory itself was profoundly influenced by the emergence of a number of writers who approached value problems from the view-point of monopoly, and emphasised the unrealistic nature of an analysis which was based on the assumptions of perfect competition and a perfect market. Most of all, however, economic thought was dominated by the desire to find a solution for the problem of how to maintain the level of effective demand so as to avoid the recurrence of phases of deep depression and widespread unemployment. There was a growing feeling of impatience with the economics of the long period "in which we are all dead," and a great, perhaps even excessive, concentration on the short period in which we live and move and have our being.

The result was a remarkable ferment of ideas, the challenging of ancient orthodoxies, and "for the moment controversy and doubt (were) increased." This ferment had by no means subsided when the second war with Germany broke out in September 1939, bringing in its train a degree of State interference with the normal peace-time working of the economic system far exceeding that reached even in the last years of the war of 1914–18.

In so far as it is possible to foresee future trends, they would seem to lie in a much greater measure of conscious public control over many aspects of economic activity than has existed in the past. It will no doubt still remain true, to quote Lord Keynes's Introduction again, that:

> "The Theory of Economics does not furnish a body of settled conclusions immediately applicable to policy. It is a method rather than a doctrine, an apparatus of the mind, a technique of thinking, which helps its possessor draw correct conclusions."

Nevertheless, economists may well find themselves to a greater degree than hitherto called upon to express their views on matters of economic policy, and—for a time at least—the writers of future volumes of the Cambridge Economic Handbooks may be concerned rather with specific problems than with the more general aspects of economic theory.

C. W. GUILLEBAUD

July 1946

PREFACE TO FOURTH EDITION

In composing a new edition of this book I have decided, after much consideration, to preserve the general framework and the order of topics intact. This has the incidental advantage that those teachers who have continued to recommend it for reading will find the expositions of the various subjects in their old places.

My main reason, however, is that I remain convinced, despite all that has happened during the last quarter of a century, that an introduction to the subject through an understanding of the law of comparative costs brings to the student's attention those things which it is most important that he should know about foreign trade. It may be that the use of such concepts as the community indifference curve brings to light certain points that slipped through the meshes of the comparative cost analysis; I believe that those are not the most important points. I would further claim that the comparative cost law, in the form in which I have presented it, is conceptually impeccable, and not open to the objections that may be raised against the earlier classical statements of it. It also provides a check, somewhat analogous to that of double entry in book-keeping, whereby some weaknesses in the arguments of those recommending tariffs as methods of improving the terms of trade can be detected.

Excitement was caused some years ago by a proposition of far-reaching import put forward by Professor Samuelson about factor price equalisation. Many economists felt that his conclusion must depend on rather special assumptions; I agree with that. Reflection upon it led me to re-consider the attempt by Professor Ohlin to re-state old doctrine by reference to the unequal endowment of different countries with general factors, such as capital and labour, taken to be required in different admixtures for the production of different commodities. I reached the conclusion that, although this was an interesting approach, such inequality in the endowment of different factors, while it might lead to great differences in the standards of living as between countries, would *not* lead to differences of comparative cost of quantitative importance. I inferred that reference to this inequality of endowment should not be taken as the main line of approach to our subject. It was accordingly with relief that, when I looked back to my own book, I found that I had based my treatment—guided, I now like to think, by a sure instinct—on the *specificity* of factors of production. If in the case of each commodity one factor is specific, Samuelson's conclusion by his own admission does not hold.

viii

I have left some passages unchanged, as being early or first statements of doctrines that have since prevailed. Those on imperfect competition (pp. 55–58 and 75–76) were composed before the well-known books by Mrs. (Joan) Robinson and Professor E. H. Chamberlin had appeared, and embodied ideas that I had previously expressed in articles. It may be that these passages gained by the doctrines being less rigidly expressed than they were in subsequent formulations. In the 1939 edition I set out (in Chapter 6) what I believe to have been the first statement of the doctrine of the "foreign trade multiplier", which is now commonly accepted.

Chapters 7 and 8 have been entirely re-written and Chapter 9 disappears. Some portions of Chapter 5 (on foreign exchange) have been dropped, and lengthy new sections added, in order to bring it up to date. An important new section has been added to Chapter 4, which provides an essential link between the pure theory of comparative costs and the price mechanism as it operates in foreign trade. Some of the tables in Chapter 2 have been altered, with a view to bringing them into stricter relation with certain specific assumptions.

While the first five chapters of this book are designed to give an account of a generally agreed system of economic doctrine, parts of the following chapters, which deal with more recent doctrines still evolving and with questions of policy connected therewith, are nesessarily more tentative, provisional, and personal to the author.

June 1957   R. F. HARROD

AUTHOR'S NOTE TO SECOND EDITION

In this revised edition Chapters VI–VIII have been completely rewritten. The theory of the balance of trade and the balance of payments has been treated more fully; and its relation to certain modern views regarding fluctuations in employment and the balance of saving and capital outlay at home expounded.

January 1939   R. F. H.

CONTENTS

CHAPTER III

POTENTIAL AND ACTUAL GAIN

CHAPTER IV

COMPARATIVE PRICE LEVELS

CHAPTER V

FOREIGN EXCHANGE

CHAPTER VI

THE BALANCE OF TRADE

CHAPTER VII

CORRECTING AN IMBALANCE

CHAPTER VIII

A REFORMED WORLD

INTERNATIONAL ECONOMICS

CHAPTER I

INTRODUCTORY

§ 1. The Scope of this Volume. It is proper at the outset to give some idea of the scope of this volume. The title does not sufficiently define it, for international economics is a large and complex subject; it might be surveyed from an historical or a geographical point of view; a brief description of the principal constituent items of international trade might be attempted; above all the reader might hope to find an analysis of the present phase and tendency of international trade, with a view to forming opinions about the probable course of events and appropriate policy. The purpose of this book is more precise and definite. As a preliminary to understanding aright the inner nature of particular events or to forming an intelligent opinion on matters of current controversy, it is necessary first to be apprised of certain simple and fundamental truths about international economic relations in general. It is to expound and elucidate these that an attempt is made here. The reader will find a treatment of what may be called the simple arithmetic of international economics. Far too much is commonly said and written in ignorance of or with complete disregard of this simple arithmetic.

The reader may console himself that the body of doctrine which he is asked to master is not a large one, nor is the intellectual effort required for the purpose great. It may be compared with that needed for the understanding of three or four theorems in elementary geometry. Yet that much effort is indispensable. The path is short but slippery. The subject is one in which fallacy and specious argumentation abound. Only by a thorough grasp of a few central propositions and of the means by which they are reached can immunity from the insidious attacks of quacks and propagandists be achieved. In pursuing a more developed branch of science, the student would not expect to be completely exempt from intellectual effort. Yet, really, the fact that the achievements of economics are exiguous and the tools used simple makes it necessary to concentrate all the more closely on what there is. Their complex technique of proof provides the conclusions of the more highly elaborated sciences with a defence against the inroads of charlatans. In economics fools are only too ready to rush in.

There has been much discussion whether economics should confine itself to the tracing of cause and effect or extend out into the practical sphere of advice and recommendation. Critics hold that, in making recommendations, economists are impinging on the region of ethics or politics. Controversy about method should, however, be settled, not on abstract grounds, but by reference to the achievements of the subject. Study of the most notable economic work reveals that it has in fact contained a large element of the practical recommendation. The objection to this rests on a misunderstanding. The phenomena studied by the economist are largely connected with human purposes, which in their interaction have given rise to a system of some complexity. When a change occurs in part of the system, it may be interesting to know, and appropriate for economists to study, what consequential changes are likely to occur in other parts of the system. It is also interesting to test the system by the criterion of how far the purposes which give rise to it find their fulfilment through it.

To test the system in this way is not to criticize the purposes themselves, which would, indeed, be an ethical matter. In studying the system, an approach may be made either by analysing the interaction of changes in its parts or by testing it with reference to its efficacy. The two approaches sometimes lead into the same terrain of analysis. It may be convenient now to adopt one, now another. Testing the system leads naturally on to making recommendations. Indeed the recommendations can often hardly be distinguished from a precise statement of how the system fails when the test is applied to it. In what follows the test method of approach is rather prominent. It is used in the analysis of the course of international trade and of the monetary system. The question is asked, what are the conditions in which trade takes such a course, that the purposes for which trade is admittedly undertaken are most fully realized? Again, what is the kind of monetary system which best fulfils the purposes for which the use of money is admittedly devised? No *a priori* justification for the procedure will be given; it has, in fact, yielded the best results in this particular field. The recommendations which rise naturally out of such an examination contain no ethical element or political bias.

The treatment of the direction and scope of foreign trade given in the early part of this volume is based on the doctrines of the classical writers. These have been subjected to much criticism in the past, mostly of a pettifogging or terminological kind; the main classical position in this sphere seems inexpugnable. The old economists were more concerned with the direction of trade than its volume. This is in line with their tendency to assume full employment at home as the normal condition and unemployment as an occasional and transitory phenomenon. Recently much work has been done on the fundamental causes of unemployment. In the second part of this volume an attempt has been made to develop a theory concerning the volume and balance of foreign trade, connecting this subject with the theory of unemployment at home. The size of this handbook has enforced strict simplicity of treatment, and this has an advantage. It is hoped that the propositions advanced throw much light on the subject, but are at the same time sufficiently elementary to be generally acceptable. An effort has been made to utilize modern theory without elaborating it so far as to take the reader on to ground which is still a field of controversy.

§ 2. International Economics as a Branch of General Economics.

International economics is concerned with all economic transactions involving passage across a national frontier. Examples are emigration, the loan of capital by the nationals of one country to those of another, the purchase of goods by the nationals of one country from those of another. A set of infinitely vigilant frontier officials might be able, by examining all persons, cargoes, and mail-bags entering or leaving Great Britain, to draw up an inventory of all the international economic transactions in which she was involved. It may at once occur to the reader that the findings of this company of officials might not be very different from those of another set whom we may imagine to have formed a cordon round the county of Warwick. They, too, would have their passengers, goods, and mail-bags to examine, and they, too, would find migration, loans, the sale and purchase of goods, etc., in progress across the boundary. The Warwickshire inventory of transactions with the outer world would be quite similar to the British inventory. Nor need we stop at the Warwickshire example. A circular cordon might be described, having Rugby for its centre and ten miles for its radius and a similar result could be achieved.

Clearly, if international economics is to be justified as a proper subject of study, it is necessary to show that the transactions entered on the British inventory have attributes which make them differ substantially from transactions recorded in any of the similar inventories which might be drawn up on boundaries *not* coincident with national frontiers. In what ways do the economic transactions between people living under different national governments differ from those between people living under the same national governments, but in different localities?

It is important not to exaggerate the differences. For instance, there is one notable respect in which the international and, may we call them, inter-county transactions do not differ, namely, that the inward payments to which all give rise must roughly balance the outward payments, the difference, if any, being covered by an actual remission of money. Theories regarding the mechanism by which the national balance of foreign payments is maintained may be tested by applying them to any arbitrarily defined area. If they implicitly assume the presence in every such area of a mechanism which does not in fact exist, they are properly suspect.

Moreover, it is also important to recognize the close inter-connexion between international and internal transactions. It would lead to disastrous errors to treat the two in watertight compartments. The state of the external world may affect not only the volume of our imports and exports, but also such apparently domestic matters as the yield of income-tax and the rate at which new houses are constructed. Special attention will be given to this interconnexion.

§ 3. **Distinguishing Features of International Transactions.** What, then, are the distinguishing attributes of the inventory of international transactions?

(i) First and foremost, attention should be paid to the migration figures, the movement of persons across the boundaries. Temporary visits need not be considered here. A number of persons born and bred in Warwickshire leave it to settle and earn their livelihood in other parts of the kingdom, and vice versa. Similarly, each year a number of persons emigrate from the kingdom to seek their fortunes in other countries. But the volume of inter-county movement, considered in proportion to the size of the area affected, is much greater than that of the international movement. Labour is more mobile between the different parts of a national unit than between different national units.

The reasons for this are sufficiently obvious. Barriers connected with language, national habits and sentiment, and, in recent times, stringent legal restrictions, obstruct the free flow of labour between different countries. The consequences are important. Within the national unit there is a tendency towards equality throughout the country in rewards to work, requiring given intensity and skill. Good opportunity for earning high rewards in one locality attracts movement to it from other parts of the country, and this movement sets up the tendency towards equalization. But great differences in the rates of reward may subsist in different countries; the general level of real wages is roughly twice as high in New York as in London, roughly twice as high in London as in Rome. Such differences could not continue long in one country. What is true of the movement of labour applies, though in less degree, to the movement of capital and enterprise.

It follows that internal trade consists largely of the interchange of goods between producers who enjoy similar standards of life. International trade often consists of the interchange of goods between producers enjoying widely different standards. It is clear that the principles which determine the course and nature of these two kinds of interchange must be in some respects different.

This is the most important circumstance which makes a special study of international trade necessary. Analysis of internal trade assumes that there is a tendency towards an equal standard of living among those doing the same kind of work. The assumption may not accord with the facts precisely, but it is a workable approximation. In the case of international trade it has to be dropped entirely. Similar standards may prevail in different countries, but there is no *a priori* probability that they will. The analysis of the advantages which accrue from international trade is independent of whether they do or not. The frequent claim that the import of goods made with cheap foreign labour should be checked thus implies ignorance of the first principles of the subject; for it assumes that inequality of wages in two competing countries is abnormal, whereas in fact it is on the probable presence of that feature that the special study of international as distinct from internal trade is founded.

(ii) Special facilities for production may differ from place to place in one country and be similar in different countries, crossing political frontiers freely. But there are certain facilities and disabilities which are co-terminous with national frontiers, namely those connected with the activities of government. The citizens of one country are subject to the same system of national and local taxation, to the same regulations for health, sanitation, factory organization, education and social insurance, the same policy with regard to transport and public utilities, the same laws regarding industrial combination and trade unions, the same commercial code. Here is another basis for the distinction between internal and international trade. Even if capital and labour flowed freely between countries so that wages, interest charges, profits, etc., were the same everywhere, the general level of real costs might be lower in one country than another, by reason of the superior advantages provided by the system of government. It would still be possible to distinguish between internal trade as interchange between producers provided by the government with similar amenities for production, and international trade as interchange between producers provided by the government with dissimilar amenities.

(iii) International transactions involving the payment of money are usually mediated by a foreign exchange transaction. Unless a common monetary standard is maintained fluctuations in the rates at which national moneys may be exchanged against each other clearly give a distinguishing mark to those transactions which are directly affected by the exchange rates.

Even if a common standard is in operation and foreign exchange fluctuations are confined within narrow limits, the fact that each national currency is controlled by its own government and central bank has special significance for international economics. The maintenance of the monetary standard involves the enforcement of a specific policy by the central bank; an identical policy is not always required in all countries at the same time. This policy has repercussions on the whole economic life of the community to whose needs the central bank is administering. National areas are usually co-terminous with those controlled by a single central banking system. Thus, from one point of view, international transactions may be thought of as the class of all economic transactions between persons living in the spheres of influence of different central banks.

CHAPTER II

THE GAIN FROM FOREIGN TRADE

§ 1. Importance of this Subject. The question which I propose to put first is, what are the advantages to be derived from foreign trade? It is convenient to do this, partly because the topic is one on which the most profound misconceptions prevail, partly because it is in its broad outline the simplest and most securely founded part of the subject of foreign trade, and also because it is well to bear the answer to this question in mind in considering and criticizing the mechanism by which foreign trade is actually carried out and all or some of its potential advantages reaped.

Much popular writing on the subject of foreign trade shows considerable knowledge about the mechanism of foreign payments, the foreign exchanges, the balance of trade and circumstances likely to affect it, but no understanding whatever of what it is all for. Without a firm grasp of the origin and nature of the advantages that accrue from foreign trade, it is not possible to say much that is sensible about it. The reader is therefore asked at the outset to follow a discussion of the precise circumstances which determine the scope and degree of gain which foreign trade can be made to yield.

§ 2. The International Division of Labour. As exchange in general is necessitated by the division of labour, so foreign trade appears when the division of labour is pushed beyond national frontiers. It is the necessary consequence of an international division of labour. Two aspects of the division of labour may be mentioned. One is the splitting up of a productive process into parts, so as to simplify and thus render more effective the work which each labourer has to perform. The other is the adaptation of the productive system so as to give the greatest possible scope to those who have special talents or facilities for doing certain kinds of work.

It might be thought that the millions of workers which most nations can claim would suffice for the bare splitting up of the whole productive complex into conveniently simple parts. Adam Smith referred to the eighteen processes involved in pin-making; this must be multiplied by an appropriate number to accord with modern conditions; but, even if we multiplied the product by the number representing all the variety of different commodities which a community needs, we should be surprised if we found more productive processes in all than the number of workers in the whole community. This, however, would not be a fair procedure. Our demand for all commodities is not equal; if the working population were divided in proportions corresponding to our demand for various products, it is possible that the number earmarked for making some product the demand for which is a minute proportion of the whole would not be sufficient to give the most economical division of labour in the making of that product. If a nation is to be self-sufficing, a large proportion of its workers must be engaged in making the main staple commodities, and the surplus left over for each of the various specialities might be inadequate, and so some international division of labour would be desirable.

By hypothesis, however, this cannot be the cause of international division of labour on a big scale. And so it is necessary to look to the other aspect of the division, namely, the convenience of setting those with special facilities to do the tasks for which they are most fitted. Let each nation produce that which it can produce most cheaply.

Whence arise these special facilities?

(i) Special facilities are provided by natural resources. Mines must be worked where they are found. This implies foreign trade, since the nations in whose territory the mines are situated must receive goods of some sort in exchange for the ores which they export. Many products, coffee, tea, rubber, etc., require a special climate for their cultivation.

Lands differ in natural fertility; it is desirable that more fertile land should be worked more intensively. This by itself might not give rise to foreign trade, for the world's population might be distributed in proportion to the fertility of land, so as to provide a dense population for the rich soils to support and a thinner layer for poorer soils. It is not, however, permissible to suppose that the population of the world is in fact so distributed.

(ii) If mother earth yielded all things in equal abundance in all her parts, the uneven distribution of population would itself make foreign trade desirable. Certain productive processes, those of the extractive industries, must needs be conducted in close collaboration with the natural resources. Others, those concerned with the working up of raw materials into finished goods, can be conducted apart. Countries with a population dense in proportion to the capacity of the soil would naturally employ their surplus on the processes which do not have to be undertaken in close conjunction with the soil, and exchange manufactured goods for the raw products of more sparsely peopled regions.

(iii) Human capacity differs as well as that of the earth. The difference may be due to innate racial qualities of manual dexterity, scientific ability, vigour and enterprise, or to the political and social structure, itself the result of racial capacity for social organization, or of the whole chain of historical accidents. Processes in which scientific skill or the capacity for conducting great collaborative enterprise—production on a large scale—counts for more in increasing efficiency should naturally be undertaken by the peoples more highly endowed with these qualities.

(iv) There is the legacy of the past. A nation may be bequeathed a great structure of equipment, of factories and railways, or with a structure of organization, special knowledge and useful habit, constituting present aids to certain forms of production. The growth of this structure may have been due to good fortune or a natural superiority in the past, now vanished. But the legacy has not vanished. The inherited structure may give special facilities, which are as decisive a factor in determining its proper sphere of specialization as the presence of mines or oil-fields. If the peculiar advantages which aided the growth of this structure cease to exist, after a very long time the structure itself will disappear, just as a coal mine is finally worked out, and the nation will ultimately take its place among other nations bereft of this distinguishing feature.

If the greatest possible advantages of foreign trade are to be secured for all, each nation should devote itself to what it can do most cheaply. The expression "what it can do most cheaply" needs careful definition.

§ 3. The Law of Comparative Costs. Writers on foreign trade have usually found it convenient to develop this definition by considering in the first instance two nations producing two commodities. An alternative method is to consider the position of one country, to be called the "home country", in respect of two commodities *vis-à-vis* the rest of the world. The principle to be defined then becomes—the home country should produce for herself and for export what she can produce more cheaply, and import from abroad what can be produced more cheaply there.

The term "abroad" is, of course, an abstraction. The outer world is not a homogeneous place but consists of a large number of particular countries, each with its own conditions. For the purpose of considering the gain from trade to the home country, it is convenient to suppose that the other countries have already entered into those trading relations which they think fit and have established some sort of equilibrium with each other, so that, for the purpose of isolating the phenomenon to be studied, we can compare the state of affairs when the rest of the world has all its complex relations but no trade with the home country, with that when the rest of the world has all its complex relations and its trade with the home country also.

It must be emphasized that this is an attempt to state what

should happen, if full advantage is to be taken of the potentialities of the international division of labour. Whether that is what *does* happen, if trade is allowed to follow "its natural course," will be considered subsequently. Moreover, it may be held that it is not always desirable to take full advantage of the potentialities of the international division of labour, that it may be better to sacrifice increments of wealth in the interests of self-sufficiency. Such a consideration is beyond the immediate matter in hand.

Since this is an attempt to define comparative cheapness of production, it is necessary to have a unit for measuring cost of production. The same unit need not, and indeed cannot, be used for measuring cost at home and abroad. Cost may be measured in terms of trouble or effort or in terms of the reward that is paid for effort; this reward may again be measured as so many baskets full of consumable goods, or as so much money. Happily for the present purpose it does not matter which method be adopted. All methods must presuppose that different kinds of cost, e.g. labour skilled and unskilled, waiting, the use of land or mines, can be measured against each other in the same country. Commodity A may take more land per unit of labour expended on it than commodity B. To compare the cost of producing A with that of producing B, we must be able to equate land to labour as elements in cost, to say that, for instance, 1 labourer per annum=100 acres per annum, or, =150 acres per annum. If the relative values of the various factors of production are determined, it is then possible to compare the cost of producing commodities A, B, C, etc., in the same country unequivocally.

The relative values of the factors may be different in different countries. Since the same unit will not be used for measuring the cost of producing commodities at home and abroad, this circumstance will not affect the argument.

To compare costs of production, units of the commodities must also be defined. Commodities are usually measured in tons, yards, etc., but for this purpose it is most convenient to take, as a unit of the commodity B, that amount of B which has in the first instance the same cost of production as a unit of the commodity A in the home country. Let us suppose that they each cost x units to produce. It is well to leave it undecided whether this means £x, x labour days, or x baskets full of commodities, etc.

Let the cost of producing a unit of A abroad be y units. The nature of the unit of cost is again left undefined. The following table represents the definitions given so far:

TABLE I

	Cost of production at home	Cost of production abroad
Unit of commodity A .	x	y
Unit of commodity B .	x	–

The unit of B was defined as that amount of B which has the same cost of production at home as that of the chosen unit of A at home. Hence if the cost of producing a unit of A at home is x, that of producing a unit of B is also x. We have next to consider the cost of producing precisely these units of A and B abroad. We have supposed the cost of producing this unit of A to be y. So far nothing has been assumed about comparative cheapness at home or abroad. This will be determined by the fourth term which has to be inserted to make the table complete.

The fourth term may be equal to, greater than or less than y. If the cost of producing the unit of B abroad is y:

TABLE II

	Cost of production at home	Cost of production abroad
Unit of commodity A .	x	y
Unit of commodity B .	x	y

no saving of cost can be gained by the home country taking on the production of either A or B for foreign consumption. It should be noted that this result has been arrived at without any assumption with regard to the relation of the cost of producing A at home to that of producing A abroad. It has not been asserted that y is equal to, less than, or greater than x; moreover, such an assertion would have been meaningless, for it is not known whether any common unit for measuring costs in the two countries can be found. If the relative values of labour, capital and land happen to be different in the two countries, no common unit is possible.

Suppose now that the "fourth term" is greater than y and equal to, say, $2y$:

TABLE III

	Cost of production at home	Cost of production abroad
Unit of commodity A .	x	y
Unit of commodity B .	x	$2y$

Productive resources can be applied with equal efficacy to the production of units A or B at home; but productive resources abroad are only half as efficacious in the production of these units of B as they are in that of these units of A. It follows from this that there will be a net increase in production if the home country takes over the production of B for foreign consumption and imports A in exchange. By transferring productive effort from B to A the foreigner produces twice as many units of A as he was producing of B; by transferring productive effort from A to B, the home country produces no less units of B than she formerly produced of A. How the benefits arising from the interchange will be distributed between the home country and the foreigner is discussed later.

But first the reader is asked to reconsider the tables, lest any misconception remain in his mind. Table III suggests, by reason of the notation adopted, that the home producer is better placed than the foreigner, because on the whole he

seems able to produce more cheaply. Nothing of the sort
has been assumed.   The units measured by x and y respectively
are different units. y might equally well have been defined as
the cost of producing a unit of B abroad.   In that case the
facts would be represented as follows:

TABLE IV

	Cost of production at home	Cost of production abroad
Unit of commodity A .	x	$\frac{1}{2}y$
Unit of commodity B .	x	y

The facts represented in Table IV are precisely the same as
those represented in Table III, though in Table IV the foreigner
has the specious appearance of being more efficient, while in
Table III it is the home producer who has that appearance.

The reason why the same facts can be represented in either
way is that no assumption has been made about whether the
home producer or the foreigner is, taking the two commodities
together, the more efficient; and the reason why no assumption
was made is that it is irrelevant to the possibility of gain by
interchange.   This gain does not depend on the comparative
cheapness of producing A at home and abroad or on the
comparative cheapness of producing B at home and abroad.
The gain depends on the relation between the ratio of the cost
of production of A to that of B at home and the ratio of the
cost of production of A to that of B abroad.   *Gain is possible
if the ratios are different.*

When trade is undertaken, the scene changes.   Each
country will come to produce more of some commodities and
less or none of others.   This will probably affect the costs of
those which she still produces.   New ratios of cost will be
established.   If these are still different from those prevailing
abroad, gain can be secured by a further expansion of trade,
and this again affects her ratios of cost.   It follows that, when
all the trade is undertaken that yields a gain, her ratios of cost

will no longer be different from those abroad. A country should expand or curtail the production of different commodities until her ratios of cost are the same as those abroad, and export the surplus or import the deficiency so generated. (In some lines production may be abandoned entirely, and some goods may be imported which were not consumed before trade was opened, owing to the excessive cost or impossibility of producing them at home.)

The principle set forth above is known as the Law of Comparative Costs and is due to Ricardo. It remains the fundamental principle in this subject.

So far costs of transport have been neglected. Gain can only occur if (adopting the notation of Table III) the cost of sending a unit of B from the home country to its foreign market plus the cost of sending that amount of A which has the same exchange value as a unit of B from its source of production to the home country is less than y. Otherwise the saving in productive costs will be swallowed up by the additional costs of transport. Any reduction in the costs of transport enlarges the sphere of gain by foreign trade. To cost of transport, excess cost of salesmanship must be added, where by excess cost of salesmanship is meant the excess, if any, of the cost of selling a unit of home-produced B to its foreign buyer over that of selling it at home, plus the excess, if any, of the cost of selling the appropriate amount of foreign-produced A to the home buyer over that of selling it abroad. For the trade to yield net advantage, the saving in productive cost must exceed both the additional transporting and selling costs. Any improvement of diplomatic relations, any tightening of non-commercial bonds of intercourse between nations, or any increase of foreign investment, will probably make it easier for a seller to establish relations with his foreign market and so enlarge the sphere of possible gain by foreign trade.

§ 4. A Method of Assessing the Gain from Foreign Trade.

The proposition that each country should produce what it can do most cheaply has now been defined. The next topic is the circumstances that determine the amount of gain which the trade yields. In the tables shown above, by "Cost of production at home" was meant the cost of producing that amount of the commodity which the home country would produce if the channels of foreign trade were closed to it. By "Cost of production abroad" was meant the cost of producing that amount of the commodity which would be produced abroad if there were no trade with the home country.

If the home country was self-contained the coal-wheat position might be illustrated by some such figures as:

TABLE V: COSTS IN NO-TRADE CONDITION

	Cost at home	Cost abroad
Unit of wheat . . .	x	y
Unit of coal . . .	x	$4y$

If in these circumstances interchange between the home country and the rest of the world becomes possible, costs can be saved if the home country produces some coal for export in exchange for wheat. If resources are transferred from the production of wheat to that of coal in the home country, the extra coal being exported in exchange for wheat from abroad, in the first instance one unit of wheat is lost for every extra unit of coal produced and exported. But for every unit by which coal production abroad is reduced, four units of wheat can be produced instead. Consequently for every unit by which wheat production is reduced in the home country, four units of wheat can be produced instead, without any detriment to the production of coal in the two regions taken together, and without the use of any more productive resources in all. Alternatively matters could be so arranged that more coal was produced without any detriment to the production of wheat and without the use of any additional productivity resources. Or, more probably, some more of both could be produced. Or again, according to taste, the two regions, not desiring so much extra wheat and coal as the interchange would allow them to have without the use of extra productive resources, might decide to direct some of the resources formerly used for wheat and coal to the production of other commodities, which would be sheer gain to them, since they would also be enjoying more wheat and coal than they had before.

There are various possibilities with regard to the way in which costs will change as the scale of output alters. In general, it is proper to suppose that the Law of Increasing Costs operates for the following reason.

Comparative costs are different in different countries because the abundance of factors especially appropriate to the production of each commodity ("specific" factors) does not bear the same relation to the demand for each commodity in different countries. Thus, in the above example, it is to be supposed that, when the home country is cut off from foreign trade, the ratio of the abundance of coal mines (relatively to the demand for coal there) to the abundance of land suitable for wheat production (relatively to the demand for wheat there) is greater than that ratio abroad. Consequently the ratio of wheat rents to coal-mining royalties will be higher in the home country than abroad, and the ratio of the amount of non-specific factors (e.g. labour) used to produce a unit of wheat to that used to produce a unit of coal will be higher at home than abroad. In these circumstances the cost of producing wheat, compared with that of producing coal, will be higher at home than abroad, as shown in Table V.

If the home country begins to produce more coal, some being for export, and less wheat, some being imported for home consumption, that will tend to make available coal deposits less abundant in relation to the demand, which is now enhanced, and wheat-fields more abundant in relation to the demand, which is now decreased. This tends to change the ratio of costs in the home country in the direction of the world ratio. By converse reasoning the world ratio will be changed in the direction of the home ratio.

Coal and wheat have been chosen in this example to facilitate thinking, but the foregoing observations with regard to the

3

relative abundance of specific factors are general and do not
apply only to the extractive industries. The various different
commodities normally require different specific kinds of skill
or "know-how" for their production. The case, however,
where there are countervailing forces which produce constant
or decreasing costs over a certain range is considered in § 9.

As the home country increases her output of coal, her cost
of coal relative to her cost of wheat rises, and as she reduces
her output of wheat, her cost falls; and as the rest of the world
increases its output of wheat, its cost of wheat relative to its
cost of coal rises. The new ratios might be as follows:

TABLE VI: COSTS WHEN SOME TRADE IS UNDERTAKEN

	Cost at home	Cost abroad
Unit of wheat .	$0 \cdot 90x$	$1 \cdot 10y$
Unit of coal .	$1 \cdot 10x$	$3 \cdot 60y$
Ratio of costs .	$9 : 11 \ (= 1 : 1 \cdot \dot{2})$	$11 : 36 \ (= 1 : 3 \cdot \dot{2}\dot{7})$

Since the ratios are still unequal and the home producer has a
comparative advantage in producing coal, something may be
gained by his taking on the production of still more coal.
The same reasoning can be used to demonstrate this as was
used in relation to Table V. He should push on with the
production of coal until the rise in his cost of producing it and
in the foreigner's cost of producing wheat and the fall in his
cost of producing wheat and in the foreigner's cost of producing
coal have brought the ratios of their costs to equality. Thus:

TABLE VII: COSTS WHEN FULL TRADE IS UNDERTAKEN

	Cost at home	Cost abroad
Unit of wheat . . .	$0 \cdot \dot{6}x$	$1 \cdot \dot{3}y$
Unit of coal . . .	$1 \cdot \dot{3}x$	$2 \cdot \dot{6}y$

Common ratio of costs: 1 : 2

The ratios now being the same in both spheres, no further
gain can be achieved by the transfer of more production.

The figures set out in Table VII show a rise in the cost of coal at home and in that of wheat abroad and a fall in the cost of wheat at home and in that of coal abroad. Many figures might have been used to illustrate these tendencies; the figures set down were not, however, chosen arbitrarily. They follow from certain assumptions selected as the simplest, and on the basis of these it is seen that gain from trade would be divided equally between the two regions. By varying the assumptions one may use this type of table to show what governs the degree and distribution of benefit from trade. The assumptions were as follows:

First, it has been assumed that the increase of the production of coal at home is equal to its decrease abroad; similarly with wheat. This is to ignore, for the time being, the effect of the opening of trade on the *demand* for these commodities. (See § 8.)

Secondly, it has been assumed that the costs of wheat and coal change in the same proportion at home and abroad, as the amount of production is varied. Thus the cost of wheat at home is made to fall by one-third and the cost abroad to rise by one-third; similarly the cost of coal at home rises by one-third and the cost abroad falls by one-third. Again, the cost of coal at home rises by the same fraction as that by which wheat falls.[1]

This assumption may be expressed by saying that cost "gradients" are proportional to costs ruling in the opening position. The height of a cost curve shows the cost per unit produced and varies according to the total amount produced.

---

[1] It might be thought that as in the new situation, when two units of wheat (as defined in Table V) exchange for one of coal, the production of two units of wheat can be abandoned at home for every extra unit of coal produced, the cost of wheat should be made to change by twice the amount that the cost of coal changes. Such an assumption would not be the most natural one. In the tables the "unit" of coal is defined by reference to cost conditions at home; it could equally well have been defined by conditions abroad. Neither has logical priority over the other. To get neutral units and thereby the most natural assumptions about how much costs change when trade is undertaken, I assume 1 unit of coal to be that amount of coal for which 1 unit of wheat is exchanged, *when full trade is undertaken*. See Appendix.

The gradient of the curve measures the rate at which the cost per unit increases as more is produced. If cost decreased, the gradient would be negative; i.e. the curve would slope downwards to the right.

Costs of wheat at home and abroad and the cost of coal abroad have changed by ·1 of a unit in Table VI and by ·3 of a unit in Table VII; the cost of coal abroad has changed by ·1 × 4 (= ·4) in Table VI and by ·3 × 4 (= 1·3) in Table VII. The multiplication by 4 is because the opening cost of coal abroad is four times as great. If we worked with the more familiar "elasticity"[1], we should have to make specific assumptions about the numbers of units of wheat and coal initially produced in each country, which would complicate the argument.

One further point must be noted here. As production changes, the relative values of the factors used in production also change. It is necessary to have some common units (x and y) for comparing costs in each country separately before and after the change. Classical writers were apt to use a labour-day. But even that is dangerous, since agricultural labour cannot be regarded as identical with coal-mining labour; consequently the reward paid for an agricultural labour-day may change relatively to that paid for a coal-mining labour-day, and consequently the amount of cost due to the employment of a labour-day in wheat production may change relatively to that due to the employment of a labour-day in coal mining. It should, however, be possible to find some factor common to both industries, such as a transport-labour-day.

Thirdly, it is assumed that trade between the two regions must balance. (This is not always assumed in introductory expositions of the law of comparative costs, and the mechanism for doing so here presented may accordingly be regarded as an improvement.)[2]

----

[1] If x is the amount produced and y the cost per unit, the cost gradient is $\frac{dy}{dx}$. The elasticity of supply in terms of cost is $\left(\frac{dx}{x} \div \frac{dy}{y}\right)$.

[2] See Appendix, pp. 182-3.

The following criteria may be adopted for comparing the degree of gain from foreign trade in various circumstances. (i) The gain will be greater the greater the volume of trade. (ii) The gain will be greater the lower the cost of producing enough coal to buy one unit of wheat at the newly established ratio by comparison with the cost before trade of producing one unit of wheat. This will partly depend on how much more favourable to coal is the rate at which it will exchange for wheat after trade, by comparison with the rate at which it exchanged for wheat at home before trade was opened. The rate, as finally established, is sometimes called the "real ratio of international interchange", or, more simply, the "terms of trade".

§ 5. Gain through Difference of Cost Ratios.   Gain by trade is possible when the initial cost ratios are different at home and abroad. It will be greater, the larger the difference is, other things being equal, e.g. the cost gradients. This may be simply illustrated by tables constructed on the same plan as V and VII.

The following table shows a more moderate disparity of initial costs:

TABLE VIII: INITIAL POSITION

			Cost at home	Cost abroad
Unit of wheat	.	.	.	x	y
Unit of coal	.	.	.	x	$2y$
Ratios of costs	.	.	.	1:1	1:2

TABLE IX: WHEN FULL TRADE IS UNDERTAKEN

			Cost at home	Cost abroad
Unit of wheat	.	.	.	$0.83..x$	$1.17..y$
Unit of coal	.	.	.	$1.17..x$	$1.66..y$

Common ratio of costs: $1:1.414..$ (or $1:\sqrt{2}$)

The following gives an example of a larger initial disparity:

TABLE X: INITIAL POSITION

				Cost at home	Cost abroad
Unit of wheat	.	.	.	x	y
Unit of coal	.	.	.	x	$5y$
Ratios of costs	.	.	.	1:1	1:5

TABLE XI: WHEN FULL TRADE IS UNDERTAKEN

				Cost at home	Cost abroad
Unit of wheat	.	.	.	$0 \cdot 62..x$	$1 \cdot 38..y$
Unit of coal	.	.	.	$1 \cdot 38..x$	$3 \cdot 10..y$

Common ratio of costs: $1:2 \cdot 236..$(or $1:\sqrt{5}$)

From a comparison of these tables with each other and with Table V we can assess the gain from trade by the two criteria mentioned in the last section.   In the first place there is more trade the larger the initial disparity of cost ratios.   Cost gradients being assumed equal for all three examples, the amount of trade flowing may be taken to be proportional to the change in costs.   Wherever we look we find a greater change of costs the larger the initial disparity.   As all the trade is gainful, we may infer that, other things being equal, the gain due to trade will be larger the greater the initial disparity of costs.

Next we must consider gain per unit of trade.   When cost changes in consequence of trade there are two forces at work. The cost of coal will rise at home when more is produced (1) because more of the non-specific factors have to be used per unit produced, and (2) because the values of the factors specific to coal production rise relatively to the non-specific factors. Similarly when less wheat is produced, its cost falls (1) because this smaller quantity can be produced with less use of the non-specific factors per unit, and (2) because the value of factors specific to wheat production will fall. How much of the rise (or fall) of cost is to be attributed to each of these two elements depends on the particular circumstances of the case.

Let us make the assumption that is *least* favourable to gain by trade. Let us suppose that the whole rise in the cost of coal is due to the need to use more factors per unit of coal produced and not at all to the rise in the prices of specific factors. In fine the cost rises exclusively because more non-specific man-hours are taken to get each ton produced and not because, the coal trade being in a booming state, all those who have special qualifications for coal production—mine workers, technicians, company managements and royalty owners—are all able to enjoy a rise of pay (by comparison with other productive factors in the country). Taking the conditions of Tables V and VII, prior to trade it was possible to get 1 unit of wheat at the cost of $1x$; by the export of coal it proves possible to get 1 unit of wheat at the cost of $\frac{1}{2} \times 1 \cdot \dot{3} x \ (=\cdot \dot{6} x)$; the latter figure ($1 \cdot \dot{3} x$) represents the cost of producing a unit of coal in the new situation, and the former ($\frac{1}{2}$) expresses the fact that for this unit 2 units of wheat can be bought abroad. Thus the cost of getting wheat by trade is only $\frac{2}{3}$ of the previous cost of producing it at home. In Table IX, where the initial disparity is less, the cost of getting wheat is down by 17%; in Table XI, where the initial disparity is greater, the cost is down by 38%. Thus it is safe to say that, other things being equal, the greater the initial disparity, the greater will be the volume of trade and the greater the gain per unit. All these reasonings apply not only to the gain accruing to the home country, but also, in like manner, to the gain accruing to "abroad".

If the rise in the cost of coal was in part due to the higher rewards paid to the factors especially qualified for coal production, the gain from trade would be greater than that shown in the foregoing paragraph. Consider the extreme case in which the method of producing coal after trade was exactly the same as before; this is sometimes expressed by saying that the "technical co-efficients" of production are rigid. There might conceivably be only one possible method of producing coal. In this case the rise in the cost of coal would be solely the consequence of specific factors claiming and getting higher pay owing to the rise in the total demand for this product. In that case the cost to the country of getting wheat in exchange for coal would, in the conditions of Table VII, be one-half of the previous cost of getting wheat. The fact that coal was more highly priced would mean that the specific coal-producing factors were taking to themselves a special share of the gain to the country. This influence making the cost of coal rise is sometimes called a "rent" element.

Finally it has to be asked how the country will be affected by the fact that the coal produced for the home market will cost more after trade is opened and the wheat still produced at home less. If "production co-efficients" are rigid and these changes of cost are solely due to changes in rewards to specific factors (rent elements) the national income will be unaffected; the changes in cost will simply reflect a re-distribution of national income as between mine-workers and agricultural labourers and other affected interests. If this re-distribution was thought a hardship, the losers could be compensated in full and the rest of the country still be better off by the whole amount of the gain from trade.

On the other hand the change in costs might be due, in whole or in part, to the use of a smaller quantity of factors per unit in the production of wheat and a larger quantity in the production of coal. The tables show a fall in the cost of wheat equal to the rise in the cost of coal. If wheat and coal bulked equally largely in the national economy, the gain would offset the loss. If coal was much more important than wheat, the loss might be greater; but in that case it is improbable that the cost gradients would be as assumed in the tables. Had we worked with equal elasticities instead of equal gradients, the rise in the cost of coal would in those circumstances probably be less per unit than the fall in wheat.

It need not be denied that there are possible circumstances in which, after all, the gain from trade would be greatly diminished. Suppose that the rise in the cost of coal was solely due to the need to use more factors of production per unit of coal when more coal was produced, while the fall in the cost of wheat was solely due to a fall in agricultural wages, rents, etc., consequent upon the diminished demand for wheat. While the argument of § 4 suffices to show that there must be some gain from trade whenever the cost ratios are unequal, the circumstances described in this paragraph could much reduce this gain.

§ 6. Another Example of the Importance of being Unimportant.[1]

If the rest of the world is a place where much more coal and wheat are produced altogether than at home, it is unrealistic to assume the cost gradients to be equal in the two regions. They are likely to be much flatter abroad. Once again it is expedient to modify our assumption of equal gradients in the direction of equal elasticities. We must presume that coal and wheat are produced from numerous different sources in numerous different regions. The reduction of coal by e.g. 100 million tons in the rest of the world would make a much smaller difference to conditions of production in any one region than the increase of production by 100 million tons would make to conditions of production in the home country. We may construct a table assuming that the rest of the world is ten times as great as the home country in the matter of coal and wheat production and that the cost gradients are consequently only one-tenth as steep.

TABLE XII: INITIAL POSITION

			Cost at home	Cost abroad
Unit of wheat	.	.	. x	y
Unit of coal	.	.	. x	$2y$
Ratios of cost	.	.	. $1:1$	$1:2$

[1] Cf. H. D. Henderson, *Supply and Demand*, ch. V, sec. 4.

TABLE XIII: WHEN FULL TRADE IS UNDERTAKEN

				Cost at home	Cost abroad
Unit of wheat	.	.	.	$\cdot694..x$	$1\cdot0306..y$
Unit of coal	.	.	.	$1\cdot306..x$	$1\cdot9388..y$

Common ratio of costs: $1:1\cdot88...$

This table is constructed on the same principles as Table IX, except that the cost gradients are only one-tenth as steep abroad. (At home the unit costs of wheat and coal both change by $\cdot306..$; the cost of wheat abroad changes by one-tenth of $\cdot306...$ and the cost of coal by one-tenth of $(\cdot306..\times2)$). Inspection of costs in the final position in the home country reveals that eighty per cent more trade is flowing than in the equilibrium shown in Table IX.[1] *Both* parties will benefit by that. Furthermore the final ratio is much more favourable to the home country than in Table IX, viz. $1:1\cdot88...$ instead of $1:1\cdot414...$ This does but conform to common sense. If Somerset were barred from trading with the rest of England and the barrier were then lifted, the other counties would doubtless gain by the fresh opportunities for interchange, but the gain to Somerset would be immensely greater. By like reasoning, if a particular country reduced its tariffs—a partial barrier to trade—the whole world would gain, but the gain to the particular country would be far greater.

It must, of course, be understood that if a particular country bulks very largely in the production of a particular commodity, as England bulked in the production of power-made goods a hundred years ago, or as Chile in nitrates before the lowering in the cost of artificial nitrates, the rest of the world may be an equal or even greater gainer by the opening of trade with that country. This may be seen if in the former analogy, instead of Somerset, the main coal-producing counties of England had been supposed to be barred off.

[1] Costs have changed by $\cdot170..$ in Table IX and by $\cdot306..$ in Table XIII. 306 is exactly 80% more than 170.

§ **7. The Gain from Trade, and Cost Gradients.** Next we may consider the relation of cost gradients to profit by trade. In general it may be said that the less the slope of the cost gradients at home and abroad, the greater the gain from trade.

Reflection unaided by numerical example may convince the reader of this. A country gains by foreign trade if and when the traders find that there exists abroad a ratio of prices very different from that to which they are accustomed at home. They buy what to them seem cheap and sell at what to them seem good prices. The bigger the gap between what to them seem low points and high points, and the more important the articles affected, the greater will the gain from trade be. If a change in the scale of production of the home country very materially alters her costs of production, so as quickly to bring them into line with foreign prices, the gain from trade is on a small scale, and is more or less fortuitous. But if when big changes are made in the scale of operations the comparative costs at home are altered little, that means that the fundamental economic structure of the country is such as to provide a permanent and solid basis for gainful trade. In this case the cost structure ruling when foreign trade is opened is not a transitory product of a variety of special causes, but is representative of the basic conditions of the country; and if this structure differs widely from the world structure, the scene is set for profitable operations on a large scale.

In the first place it is clear that the flatter are the gradients of costs, both at home and abroad, the larger will the volume of gainful trade be. The ratios at home and abroad start a certain distance apart; the more slowly relative costs alter, whether at home or abroad, as production is switched from one commodity to another, the longer will it take for the ratios to come together.

Gain in this context is quite unequivocal. We say that there is greater gain if in the two regions together more coal and wheat can be produced with the same quantity of productive resources, or, alternatively, a greater quantity of productive resources can be released, the production of coal and wheat being held constant.

When greater gain accrues there is more gain available for both countries.   If we compare two situations in the former of which the cost curves have certain gradients and in the latter of which the home country has steeper gradients than in the former, but the rest of the world has the same gradients, more gain will be potentially available for both parties in the former situation than in the latter.

There are circumstances, however, in which the gain accruing to the home country will be greater in the latter than in the former situation.   The "terms of trade" will be more favourable to the home country in the latter situation.   In most cases this will be more than offset by the volume of trade being smaller.

J. S. Mill, in his famous essay on the Laws of Interchange between Nations, has guided subsequent writers along a wrong path by using words which focus attention on how the influence of reciprocal supply and demand affects the ratio of interchange to the neglect of this effect upon the volume of gainful trade.

Table XIV (below) may be compared with Table XIII.   It is assumed that the opening ratios are 1:1 and 1:2, that the cost gradients abroad are the same as in Table XIII but that those at home are twice as steep.   The full trade position would be as follows:—

TABLE XIV

	Cost at home	Cost abroad
Unit of wheat . . .	$\cdot68..x$	$1\cdot016..y$
Unit of coal . . .	$1\cdot32..x$	$1\cdot968..y$

Common ratio of costs: $1:1\cdot94$

The ratio is somewhat more favourable to the home country, at $1:1\cdot94..$ instead of $1:1\cdot88...$ But the amount of trade flowing, which may be measured by observing the change in cost abroad (cost gradients abroad being the same in both tables) is barely more than half (viz. $\cdot016..$ compared with $.0306..$).

If, however, we take the case when "at home" and "abroad" are equipollent, there is more chance of the home country gaining by having steeper gradients. Table XV should be compared with Table IX. The opening ratios are still 1:1 and 1:2, but "at home" and "abroad" are taken to be of equal size. The home gradients are twice as steep as those abroad.

TABLE XV

			Cost at home	Cost abroad
Unit of wheat	.	.	$\cdot 772 \ldots x$	$1 \cdot 114 \ldots y$
Unit of coal	.	.	$1 \cdot 228 \ldots x$	$1 \cdot 772 \ldots y$

Common ratio of costs: $1 : 1 \cdot 59 \ldots$

50% more trade is done in Table IX than in Table XV,[1] but the gain per unit of trade may be reckoned as $42\frac{1}{2}\%$ greater in Table XV than in Table IX.[2]   The fact that only two-thirds as much trade is done owing to the home gradient being steeper more than outweighs the fact that the gain per unit is $42\frac{1}{2}\%$ greater. But the home country could have a net advantage through having steeper gradients, provided that the steepness is not too great and that the rest of the world is not too big.

This is connected with the question of the possibility of securing net gain by imposing a tariff.   By so doing a country can always turn the terms of trade in her favour.   But only if the rest of the world is small is the gain due to this likely to exceed the loss due to the reduction in the volume of trade caused by the tariff. These matters are further discussed in the Appendix.

§ 8. The Gain from Trade, and Demand.

The next point to be considered in connexion with Table VII is its relation to the question of *Demand*.   It was assumed that in equilibrium there was the same total output of wheat and coal, the foreign increase of wheat production merely offsetting the home

[1] Viz. $\cdot 176$ compared with $\cdot 114$.
[2] Viz. $\cdot 590$ compared with $\cdot 414$, cf. Appendix, p. 184.

decrease, and the foreign decrease of coal offsetting the home increase. Changes in demand were neglected.

When demand is taken into account, it appears that the volume of trade will exceed the volume of output transferred. The import of wheat will be equal to the reduction of the home output plus the increase of home demand. The export of coal will be equal to the reduction in foreign output plus the increase of foreign demand. This introduces a new factor in the estimation of gain from foreign trade. Some of the output of coal for foreign consumption is used to buy not the wheat which we no longer produce for ourselves but additional wheat which we could only have produced at a higher cost than x. Since the transfer of demand is voluntary the consumer's surplus on the additional consumption of wheat must exceed that on the consumption of coal sacrificed. Thus when demand is taken into account, the gain from foreign trade is seen to be greater than at first appeared.

The steeper the gradient of demand, the less the volume of trade will be. If demand were absolutely inelastic the volume of trade would be no greater than the volume of output transferred from one country to another. The lower the gradient of demand, the more the volume of trade will exceed the volume of output transferred, and the greater the quantum of trade on which the gain per unit is realized.

Thus, as in the case of supply, so in the case of demand, the lower the gradients of the curves the greater the potential gain. This applies to home demand, no less than to foreign demand. But a greater steepness of the home demand, given the gradients of the foreign demand, will make the terms of trade more favourable to the home country; as with supply, this will bring net advantage to the home country only in certain circumstances, and is not likely to do so if the outer world is a large place compared with the home country.

§ 9. Foreign Trade under Constant or Decreasing Costs. How does all this analysis apply, if the operation of the Law of Increasing Costs is no longer assumed? In the first place it may be observed that its operation is by no means confined to the extractive industries. Technical skills, engineering know-how, adaptability to certain types of organization, adequate supplies of appropriate materials in proximity, knowledge about world markets for products, in fact all the circumstances which make one country more fitted than another to produce particular commodities, are usually specific to those commodities. If the production of a commodity in which a country has comparative advantage is increased, the supplies of these specific factors tend to exhaustion; their prices rise, and the amounts of each available for application per unit of output fall, so that more of the non-specific factors have to be used. Constant or decreasing costs may possibly prevail over a certain range of output; beyond it increasing costs are apt to supervene.

It is proper here to mention the class of costs, which simulate but are not identical with increasing costs of production, that Professor Robinson has called costs of growth.[1] For the purposes of this study the presence of these costs may be regarded as involving increasing costs of production; an industry subject to them may ultimately be able greatly to increase its output without a rise in cost; in an ordinary long period, expansion is limited by the rising costs of growth; these, like increasing costs proper, serve to bring cost ratios in different countries to equality.

If, on the opening of trade, the output of B at home (the export goods in Table III) enters a range of decreasing costs, production will slither along the whole of that range until increasing costs supervene. The average cost gradient between the position with no trade and the final position of equilibrium is in this case very low, being negative over part of its range, and the home country gains accordingly from the large volume of trade.

If, however, the range of decreasing costs is sufficiently extensive, the home country may be able to produce so much B before her domestic ratio of costs becomes equal to the

[1] Robinson, *Structure of Competitive Industry*, ch. VIII.

world ratio, that she can buy all the A she requires by exporting B and the production of A at home will be abandoned
altogether.   A more common case in practice is for A to be
subject to constant costs backwards from the initial position
and its production abandoned for this reason, as when an
under-developed country enters into world trade and gives up
its production of certain rudimentary processed goods.   When
the production of one commodity is abandoned, the rule that
the ratios of costs within and without must be equal will
apply in the negative sense that there will be no inequality,
since there will be no ratio at home.   The home country will
satisfy all her demand for A by exchanging B for it, at whatever
the world ratio is after trade has been opened.

In the theory of ideal competition there must be increasing
costs in equilibrium; when an industry enters upon a range of
decreasing costs, it should slither along the whole of that range
and come to rest when increasing costs again supervene.   In
practice it is found that this is often not so, and a theory to
cover cases when competition falls short of the ideal has
accordingly been developed.   The relation of this to foreign
trade is briefly discussed in the next chapter.

§ **10. A Multiplicity of Commodities Introduced.**   In the real
world there are more than two commodities entering into
foreign trade.   Inspection of A and B in isolation (Table III)

TABLE III (*repeated*)

	Cost at home	Cost abroad
Unit of A	x	y
Unit of B . . .	x	$2y$

suggested that the home country should export B in exchange
for A.   When other commodities are taken into account it
appears that this may not be desirable.   For instance:

TABLE XVI

				Cost at home	Cost abroad
Unit of A .	.	.	.	x	y
Unit of B .	.	.	.	x	$2y$
Unit of C .	.	.	.	x	$2 \cdot 5y$
Unit of D .	.	.	.	x	$3y$
Unit of E .	.	.	.	x	$5y$
Unit of F .	.	.	.	x	$10y$

If these are all the commodities there are, it is certain, assuming that transport costs are not excessive, that the home country will export F and import A. That she will export B, as seemed likely when the veil was only drawn from two commodities, now seems extremely unlikely. Though the home country has an advantage in making B compared with A, she is at a disadvantage in B compared with C, D, E and F. Which, if any, of the commodities, E, D, C and B, the home country will export depends on the importance of each and on the gradients of the supply and demand of each at home and abroad. All we can predict is that, if the maximum advantage of foreign trade is taken, the ratios in the two regions will be equal after trade has been opened and that, if the rest of the world is much larger than the home country, this ratio will resemble the right-hand ratio of Table XVI ($1:2:2 \cdot 5:3:5:10$) more nearly than the left-hand ratio ($1:1:1:1:1:1$).

§ 11. An Alternative Approach.

The foregoing exposition of the law of comparative costs was based on the idea that each commodity requires for its production one or more factors that are specific to it: trade is profitable when, as between two countries, the amounts of each specific factor with which they are endowed are not in proportion to their respective demands for the commodity to which each relates. In recent years an alternative approach has been made popular by Professor Ohlin: he takes the case of two homogeneous factors both required for two commodities, but not in the same proportions; if one country is more highly endowed with one of the factors, trade will cause it to concentrate on the commodity requiring a higher proportion of that factor. This is no doubt correct, and the situation would lend itself to analysis by tables of the type furnished above; as a country more highly endowed with capital took to producing more of the commodities requiring a higher proportion of capital, the relative price of capital would rise and with it the relative cost of the "capital-intensive" commodities the production of which was expanding. I believe that it will be found that the unequal endowment with non-specific factors will never give rise to very big differences of comparative cost—to differences big enough, for example, to cover substantial international transport costs. This is not to impugn the theory as such, but only to cast doubt on the quantitive importance of the phenomena to which it relates. Accordingly it does not seem suitable to make the unequal endowment of countries with non-specific factors the main foundation of the theory of international trade.

More recently Professor Samuelson has moved one stage further on this approach and argued that, save in the case where the rewards, or prices, of the two factors were equal in the two countries, each country would be led by trade to specialize totally on the commodity requiring more of the factor in which it was more heavily endowed. This does not seem to accord well with experience. It assumes ideal competition, which may not prevail, but it has a more radical defect. Professor Samuelson assumes that, as between commodities A and B, if A requires more capital than B per unit of labour engaged, when capital and labour have certain degrees of relative abundance (and relative prices or availabilities), A will also require more capital than B *whatever* the degrees of relative abundance of capital and labour. This assumption has no prior probability in its favour, and does not seem likely to be realized in practice as a general rule. Thus a country very short of capital may use more capital in agriculture—where waiting for the harvest is inevitable—than in textiles, where domestic spinning wheels and hand-looms may be used; a country where capital is somewhat more abundant will adopt power-driven machinery and factory organization in textiles and may well use more capital per unit of labour in textiles than in agriculture; a country still richer in capital may mechanize its agriculture and use a higher proportion of capital there than in textiles. The assumption becomes even less plausible when it is recognized that there are many factors required for production and that consequently the assumption of the more preponderant use of one factor throughout the whole range of factor prices has to apply as between any pair of factors out of all the factors. Thus while Professor Samuelson's conclusion is of interest as what is sometimes called in economics a *curiosum*, it does not seem that it should be ranked as a basic principle in this subject.

§ **12. Conclusions.**   (i) The leading principle of this chapter is that the gain from trade will be greater the more the ratios of the costs of production at home and abroad differ, when the home country and the rest of the world are cut off from one another.   Relative improvement of productive efficiency in the outer world at producing the goods which she imports redounds therefore to her advantage; an improvement in making the goods which she exports redounds therefore to her disadvantage.

(ii) The bigger the rest of the world is relatively to the home country, the greater the gain from trade.   A general improvement in productive efficiency all round in the outer world, or a growth of population, redounds therefore to her advantage. When the improvement in the outer world is concentrated upon goods which the home country exports the tendencies set out here and in (i) above are in conflict, and nothing can be said *a priori* about whether such an improvement will yield a balance of advantage for the home country.

(iii) Any reduction in transport costs or in the difficulty of selling in foreign markets or in the difficulty which a foreigner has in selling in the markets of the home country enlarges the possible sphere of gainful foreign trade.

(iv) The lower the gradients of the demand and cost curves over the relevant range of output, the greater the gain from foreign trade.[1]

These are the principal circumstances which determine whether and in what degree gainful foreign trade is possible. Our next question is—in what circumstances does the potentiality become an actuality?

---

[1] This is true unless the home country approaches the rest of the world in size, when, in certain circumstances, there may be a net advantage to the home country in having steeper demand and cost gradients.

CHAPTER III

POTENTIAL AND ACTUAL GAIN

§ **1. Two Problems.**   The last chapter was concerned with the fruits which can be reaped if the international division of labour is carried out on the right lines.   It was an account of the direction which trade ought to take, or, what is the same thing, of the way in which countries ought to dispose of their productive resources.

The question which naturally seems to arise in succession to this is—do countries in fact tend to distribute their productive resources in this way and so gather in to the full the harvest which international division of labour is capable of yielding?   What is the mechanism which would allow them to do so?

The answer which the classical writers gave to these questions was simple.   Full advantage will in fact be taken of the international division of labour, if no artificial obstacles are put to the free flow of trade, if producers and merchants are allowed and encouraged to sell where they can get the highest price and buy where they find the lowest.   It will be necessary to examine the presuppositions on which this simple answer rests.

Meanwhile there is another problem with which the classical economists did not concern themselves.   The question which interested them was—what is the best way to distribute the employment of labour and other productive services among different occupations?   There is the further question—what are the conditions in which these productive services will be fully employed?   It is now generally recognized that the volume as well as the nature of employment in the country is affected by international conditions.   It will be necessary to explore the relation of the volume of employment to the international situation.

§ 2. Three Conditions necessary for Maximizing Gain by Trade.

The present chapter is concerned with the former of these problems. It is convenient to confine the field of enquiry to the best employment of productive resources in any one country. What is said of one country will apply to each and every country and, so, to the world as a whole consequentially. Attention is also confined to the production of goods which are capable of being exported and imported and will in future be called tradable goods. The distribution of employment between tradable goods industries and other industries will be discussed subsequently.

If complete freedom of trade is allowed the prices of tradable goods in the country will not stand above their prices at any point outside by more than the cost of transporting them from that point to the country and the cost of establishing contact between the foreign seller and the domestic buyer, nor stand below their prices outside by more than the cost of carrying out the opposite operations. This condition, consequent upon free trade, may be called, briefly, the equality of prices at home and abroad.

It should be observed that, while this condition is consequent upon free trade, free trade is not necessary to it. For instance, if all foreign trade was concentrated in the hands of an Export Board and an Import Board, they could arrange that it proceeded on the right lines. They would have to push exports and allow imports on such a scale that the ratios between the home costs of producing various commodities were equal to the ratios of the foreign offer prices on the frontier of competition wherever, in equilibrium, that frontier might be. In one respect this controlled system would allow greater latitude than the free trade system. The absolute level of prices at home might be higher or lower by any amount than the absolute level abroad, provided that equality in the ratios was secured. Unfortunately the proposers of this kind of control do not make it plain that this would be the basic principle guiding operations.

If the free trade condition is realized the two following

conditions require also to be realized to secure the best international division of labour from the point of view of the country:

(i) The rewards charged by factors of production for services embodying a given degree of effort and skill must be the same in different occupations;

(ii) Producers must be willing to push production of their various wares to the point at which the money costs of production are proportional to the prices which they can obtain.[1] If these two conditions are realized, the prices at which producers are willing to offer their various wares will be proportional to the real costs of production. If the free trade condition is also realized, the production of various wares will be pushed up to the point at which the ratios of the real costs of production of the various goods are equal to the ratios of the prices of the various goods in the world generally.

But we have seen that the best division of labour is secured if the ratios of the real costs of production are the same in different countries. This in turn will be secured if the producers in each country push production up to the point at which the real cost of production ratios are equal to the world price ratios. Things equal to the same thing are equal to one another. If the real cost ratios are in each country equal to the common price ratio, they will be equal to one another. And that is the condition for the best distribution of productive resources.

It may be observed that the prices of tradable goods in different countries are not, in the free trade conditions, absolutely equal, but may differ within the limits imposed by transporting and marketing costs. But precisely this difference between real cost ratios in the various countries was laid down in the foregoing chapter as being consistent with the best distribution of productive resources.

The two subsidiary conditions for the best utilization of productive resources are general, apply over the whole field

---

[1] These two conditions really reduce to one, if producers (or entrepreneurs) are regarded as one factor of production.

of economics and are not in any sense special to the resources which enter into foreign trade. The direct proportion between the marginal utility in enjoying and the marginal disutility in producing various commodities, which in a money economy is achieved by making price correspond to cost of production, is the general condition for the best distribution of productive resources among various occupations. Correspondence of price with real cost means that the factors of production are getting the same reward in different fields; the consumer is paying them the same amount for their services whether they are making, say, boots, or motor-cars; the marginal utility which the consumer is deriving from their services is the same in different fields; no gain can therefore be made by transferring their services from one field to another. But if the rewards are different in different fields, higher, perhaps, in the production of cars than in that of boots, that is a sign that the marginal utility derived from a unit of service is higher in the case of cars than in that of boots, and that a gain could consequently be made by transferring some amount of service from the latter to the former until the rewards are reduced to equality.

A trade can only raise its rates of rewards above those of its neighbours by stinting the public of its services. Cannot it improve its relative position, it might be objected, by superior efficiency? Certainly. Managerial skill and other forms of special skill must be counted among the factors. In the ideal equilibrium, a trade conducted with higher managerial skill should show higher profit to the manager than those conducted with less. What the principle demands is that trades conducted with equal efficiency should show equal profits and rates of pay generally, and it is a platitude to remark that in the real world this is often not so. Whenever trades with equal efficiency show unequal rates of pay the public would gain by an increase in the scale of operations of one and a decrease in the other. If the rates of pay to all the factors are equal, the price, which is the sum total of the rewards to all the factors, must be proportional to cost.

A failure to adjust resources in this way necessarily means loss of national income, whether the commodities involved are those which enter into international trade or not.   There is, therefore, no need to labour this principle further.   A nation may be devoting too much attention to her exports or to some particular line of exports, or too little; the test is whether wages and other rates of pay are below or above those prevalent elsewhere.

§ 3. Fulfilment of Conditions Abroad not Essential.   Since we are considering not the best distribution from the world point of view, but how any particular country can, taking the conditions in the outer world as given, best utilize her resources, the question of the conformity between the foreign cost structure and the world price structure becomes irrelevant. The best that a particular country can do for herself is to make her own price structure correspond to her own cost structure and to enter into such foreign trade as is consistent with that condition and with the prevailing world price structure.   In a general way she gains and loses nothing by discrepancies between the world price structure and the world cost structure. That is the affair of the world; each foreign country will be better off the less her own discrepancy is.   The home country is indirectly concerned only in this way, that, according to the second conclusion of Chapter II, anything which makes the world richer will probably increase the benefits which she is in a position to derive from foreign trade.

The home country, viewing the prospects of foreign trade, is like the scientist studying nature.   He is concerned with phenomena, with the external world as it impinges on his senses; with changes of structure which can in principle have no effect on the world of experience, he has no concern.   The trader's world of experience is the actual price structure of foreign countries.

Consider the case of what is called Dumping, the habit of selling abroad below the cost of production.   Any habit which causes violent fluctuations in the foreign price structure certainly does affect the home country adversely. Each and every country is concerned to prevent situations in which producers find it profitable to make big changes in their selling prices, which have no relation to the long period trend. But in so far as the Dumping is a permanent habit, the home country can regard a sustained offer of goods by foreigners at prices below the cost of production, precisely as if the low price were due to low cost. The low price has the same effect on her whether the cause be low cost or policy.

If the Dumping has the effect of making the foreign price structure less like her own insulated cost structure, it is advantageous to her; if more like, disadvantageous. Roughly, the Dumping of goods upon her is likely to be advantageous, in that it enlarges the sphere of gainful foreign trade, while the Dumping of goods by competitors in her export markets is likely to be disadvantageous. Similarly, with regard to the products of foreign "sweated labour."

Foreign bounties or Protection have analogous effects. Protection to a particular commodity, while raising its price in the protected area, tends to make its open market world price fall. The goods which the output of the industries fostered by the foreign country displace have to find a market elsewhere or general production outside the protected area must be reduced. Both will probably happen. If this occurs in a commodity which the home country normally imports, she will gain, if in one which she normally exports, she will lose.

§ 4. Failure of Conditions: (a) When Industries are Growing or Declining. Free trade in conjunction with the two subsidiary conditions secures the best distribution of productive resources. In the following paragraphs something is said of the general circumstances likely to disturb the subsidiary conditions.

(i) Inequality of rewards in different occupations is a symptom that the transfer of productive resources from one trade to another is desirable. This may be due to a variety of reasons, a change in the world price structure, in the home

demand, or in the technical efficiency of industries. The
first sign that the transfer is desirable is a rise in the profits of
the industry to which the transfer should be made or a depression in the profits of those from which it should be made,
or both. The reward to the entrepreneurs in the two fields
thus becomes unequal. This is necessary in a system of
individualism to encourage entrepreneurs in one field and to
discourage them in another. The greater the temporary
disparity between profits, the more rapid is likely to be the
transfer of attention from one field to the other.

It is sometimes thought that, owing to the sluggishness and
conservatism of human nature, the natural incentive to shift is
insufficient to make the shift occur as quickly as it is desirable
that it should. This might be a reason for increasing the
incentive artificially by giving bounties or Protection to the
prosperous industry. The policy here suggested is to foster
the strong in order to accelerate their growth and squeeze out
the weak more rapidly.

Against this it may be urged that there is danger in such a
policy, since time is required to show whether the change in
circumstances which engendered the prosperity is to be permanent. A reckless transfer of resources to and fro would be
wasteful. The tardiness of entrepreneurs may not be more
than prudent caution requires. It should also be remembered
that profit derived from the use of existing plant is sheer gain
and that, so long as liquid resources used in conjunction with
the plant are earning their proper rate of reward, the plant
should continue to be exploited. The low rate of profit is
naturally a grievance to the owners of the plant. Nothing
should be done to encourage these owners to produce more
since their plight is a symptom that it will soon be desirable
for some of their productive resources to be transferred to other
industries.

While profits are high in one field and low in another,
pressure may be brought to bear to alter wages and salaries,
by the wage- or salary-earners in one case and by the entrepreneurs in the other. If this is carried out, a discrepancy

between comparative real costs and comparative prices arises, the money costs in the prosperous field are higher and in the depressed field lower in proportion to the cost in terms of the amount of the factors of production used. While this disparity exists, the weak trade is artificially fostered and allowed to drag out its declining career longer than it otherwise would. This discrepancy represents a further failure to make an immediate transfer of productive resources to their most profitable point of operation. If low wages are in the export trades, unprofitable foreign trade is being maintained in the wake of opportunities of profit now vanished; if in the internal trades, insufficient advantage is being taken of the opportunities in the foreign field.

The shifting of rates may be due to the prevalence of a good level of employment in the prosperous field and of unemployment in the depressed one. If there is an actual shortage of hands in the good field the shift may be desirable as being the only method of stimulating the transfer of workmen. It is analogous to the shift in comparative profits.

It might be urged that even in these circumstances the shift in rates is a sign of undesirable sluggishness on the part of the wage-earners, on the ground that the mere offer of employment in the improving field should be enough to attract the unemployed from the depressed occupation. But a change of occupation has its sacrifices and, if that is so, it is not desirable to make the change unless there is an increment of income to compensate for those sacrifices. If in these circumstances a shift in wage rates is necessary to induce the change, while the discrepancy lasts the nation is losing in production, since the high price asked by the prosperous trade to cover high wages is unduly restricting the home or foreign demand for its wares, and the low price which the depressed trade is able to ask unduly expands the demand for its; but this loss is offset by the saving of sacrifice in the troublesome and painful process of transfer, which, it may be, can be conducted with a smaller aggregate of disutility in leisure than in haste.

A discrepancy of wage rates when there is unemployment

in both fields seems less easy to justify. It is only justifiable at all in so far as it stimulates transfer. But a relatively high wage rate in the prosperous field, combined with some measure of unemployment, is hardly likely to act as a strong stimulus. A relatively high rate of reward for any factor in an occupation is justified so long as there is a shortage of the factor there, both as a necessary check to the demand for the commodity and an attraction inducing more of the factor to come from elsewhere. But, if there is unemployment in that field in addition to that due to normal seasonal fluctuation or the shifting of employment between various firms, the higher rate is probably objectionable.

Broadly, in the world at large, there has for some time been, and will continue to be, a shift away from agriculture. The reason for this is, as Mr. Loveday has so well shown,[1] that as people grow rich they spend a smaller proportion of their income on food. The capacity of the stomach is limited. The amount of food consumed continues to increase, but it increases at a lower rate than that of other commodities. If the birth rate among agriculturists is not lower than the average, men must be continually dragged out of agriculture into other occupations. This has been to some extent offset in the past by the slower rate at which productive efficiency in agriculture has increased, but with modern methods this increase will be speeded up. Consequently there has been a tendency for agricultural wages, at least in the old countries, to stand permanently below those of manufacturing industry—for the shift over is a continuous one. Thus agriculture is permanently stimulated to produce more than its correct output, by the comparative bounty to it provided by the low wages prevalent in it. There is thus a prima facie case for giving some compensating artificial stimulus to manufacturing industry in general, especially in countries which are not already encumbered by an intense manufacturing development. In countries which are highly industrialized, it is believed, reasonably or unreasonably, that it is desirable to keep a certain proportion of the population

[1] *Britain and World Trade*, passim.

on the land and that this outweighs the gain which would be derived from further industrialization.

If the shift away from agriculture required for the proper distribution of productive resources in the world becomes larger, the discrepancy between rewards in agriculture and those elsewhere will increase also. In the upward phase of the trade cycle (and in periods of post-war reconstruction) secular movements of decline are usually lost sight of, while they are accentuated in the downward phase. A crisis in agriculture and a collapse in agricultural prices may be expected to be regular features of the downward phase of the trade cycle in future, unless some other means be found for securing a quicker shift over in productive resources, or the trade cycle be eliminated.

The production of raw materials is likely to have a similar fate. Increased wealth not only involves an increase in the bulk of raw materials but also an increase in the degree to which they are worked up. This in turn means that a larger proportion of mankind will be needed for the finishing processes. Technical improvements in the utilization of raw materials may lead in the same direction. The production of consumable necessities may yield to that of quasi-luxuries. Within the sphere of quasi-luxuries there will be much more shifting about of demand than in the old more indigent days. The last-mentioned type of shift, however, is different from the others we are discussing, since its consequences are transitory and irregular. The shifts from one broad class, such as foodstuffs or raw materials, to another are enduring and likely to set up permanent discrepancies between rates of pay in different occupations. These discrepancies, which, for short, we may call wage discrepancies, have an appropriate effect in stimulating the transfer of labour and an inappropriate effect in limiting the transfer of enterprise. Whether they should be encouraged or discouraged depends on the circumstances of the case, on how necessary and effective they are in the matter of producing the movement of labour. In so far as they are judged necessary there is a case for giving an offsetting artificial inducement to the producers who are engaged in the growing branches of industry, and for giving an additional squeeze to those who are being squeezed out by the natural progress of events.

§ 5. Failure of Conditions: (b) Monopoly.

(ii) Prices may fail of adjustment to comparative real costs, because the factors have opportunities for organizing themselves better in one occupation than another, and so for securing better rates of reward. Discrepancies arising for this reason are wholly injurious, in that they deflect the employment of productive resources from the right channels.

(iii) Prices may also fail of adjustment to comparative real costs, because the monopolistic or quasi-monopolistic character of a certain industry enables the employers to hold prices above costs. This circumstance may not be unconnected with the disparities in wage rates mentioned in paragraph (ii) above, the men being able to stand out for higher rates in the quasi-monopolistic trades. Classical writers on economics were in the habit, when discussing monopoly, of dismissing it as an exceptional phenomenon. This attitude is out of date for two reasons, first because of the great growth since their day of monopolistic combinations of various kinds, whether mergers, trusts, cartels or gentlemen's agreements, and secondly because the theoretic analysis of monopoly and competition has revealed that both monopoly and competition are limiting concepts, abstractions, relating to conditions not always realized in practice, and that most industries work in conditions which are an admixture of those represented by the two concepts. Thus a large sphere which the classical writers thought of as competitive is in fact only so in a partial sense.

The ideal of competition tends to be realized in the case of completely standardized commodities in which the market is fully organized and the individual producers many and unorganized. In this case an individual throws his produce on the market in the confident expectation that he will get the ruling price for it and that his contribution will not have a discernible effect on that price. It is in his interest to push his production up to the point at which its cost is equal to the prevailing price.

True monopoly, on the other hand, is realized when a single firm, by the possession of a state grant or patent, or of the whole of the available supplies of a limited natural product, or in virtue of its immense size and commensurate resources, which enable it easily to buy off any competitor who is not prepared to operate on a similar scale, has absolute control over the whole market. Such a firm pushes its production not to the point at which its cost is equal to the price, but only to the point at which its cost is equal to the increment of receipts due to the marginal product.[1] The price exceeds the increment of receipts in the case of the monopolist, for, since he is the sole supplier, a discernible increase of his output has a discernible effect on the market price. It will depress the market price by an amount which depends on the elasticity of demand. But this depression in the price affects the whole of the rest of his output. By increasing his supply he has injured his own market. The increment of receipts due to this extra output is not the price of this increment of output at the new price level, but the price of this less the difference between the price at which he used to sell the rest of his output and the price at which he now has to sell it. He will not produce this extra output unless the increment of receipts, so measured, which is due to it, covers the cost of making it. The less elastic the demand, the more the price exceeds the increment of receipts and consequently of cost. The monopolist is always limited in his attempt to mulct the consumer by the elasticity of demand. Happily the demand for most commodities has a considerable degree of elasticity owing to the availability of substitutes. Traffic may desert the railways and take to the roads; electricity may be used instead of gas, etc.

[1] For industries subject to decreasing costs, marginal cost must be submitted for cost in this sentence; total cost per unit will be somewhat higher than marginal cost, but it will still stand below the price, if the quasi-monopoly allows abnormally high profit to be made. (Total cost per unit, or, as more briefly expressed in the text throughout, cost, is taken to include a normal rate of profit for the entrepreneur.)

Few producers have an absolute monopoly; but less producers than used to be supposed work in conditions of ideal competition. Any condition in which a producer cannot increase sales without making a price concession implies partial monopoly. This may arise in two ways, either by adhesion to an agreement among the producers, or because the market is not completely organized or the product not standardized.

In both these cases price will stand above the increment of receipts due to an increment of output. But the cost will be equated, so far as the producer's knowledge of his own cost and market conditions enables him to equate it, to the increment of receipts.[1] Consequently the price will stand above the cost of production. Producers will often fail to act in their true interest, but we may assume that their efforts to do so will lead to an even distribution of their errors around the point of their true interest, and the principle that the cost shall be equal to the increment of receipts, if not verified in the case of each individual, may be accepted as a statistical law.

Under this head the discrepancy between price and cost will be greater, the more important the element of goodwill, the more specialized and individual the product and the less organized the market. The greater the discrepancy, the more output will fall below the level required if productive resources are to be distributed in the right way.

Whether anything can be done to whip these partial monopolists into greater activity in an individualist economy is a question difficult to answer.

§ 6. Summary.

To resume the main thread of argument. In Chapter II it was laid down that, to gain full advantage of international division of labour, real cost ratios must be the same in all countries. In the present chapter it has been argued that the most any particular country can do is to make her real cost ratios correspond to world price ratios.

[1] For the modification required in this proposition in the case of decreasing cost industries, see p. 50, footnote.

This correspondence will be effected if three conditions are realized.

(i) The price ratios must be the same inside as outside the national frontiers (the Free Trade condition).

(ii) Rewards to factors must be the same in different occupations.

(iii) Producers must be prepared to sell their wares at prices proportional to the money costs of production.

Something has been said of the general circumstances which are likely to cause a failure of the second and third conditions.

CHAPTER IV

COMPARATIVE PRICE LEVELS

§ **1. A Classification of Goods.** In Chapter III two questions were put. One, dear to the heart of classical economists, was, what is the best distribution of a nation's productive resources among different occupations? The other was, what are the circumstances in which a nation will be able to make full use of her productive resources? Before the second question can be answered some consideration must be given to the relation of national price levels to each other. For the purpose of this study it is convenient to make a threefold classification of goods. The division sketched out below has, like all such divisions, an arbitrary element. Many similar divisions might be made. In the attempt to analyse a highly complex phenomenon some arbitrary simplification is inevitable.

A. The first division of goods, called briefly A goods hereafter, are the staple goods of homogeneous character and capable of entering into foreign trade. This class consists in the main of raw materials and foodstuffs. The rates at which such goods exchange for each other are, with due allowance for the costs of transport, common throughout the world. Gold is such a commodity. If we take price to be the exchange value measured in terms of gold, these goods have a single international price level. The prices of silver, copper, wheat of specific quality, rubber, tea, etc., are telegraphed from market to market and, if the price of an ounce of silver in London differs from its price in New York by more than the cost of transporting that ounce one way plus that of transporting its price in gold the other, that difference is at once corrected by an arbitrage operation. If the price of silver is higher in London, it is simultaneously offered for sale in London and purchased in equal quantity in New York, until its price is brought to an equality in the two centres. The same is true of all staple goods for which an organized market exists in the important commercial centres throughout the world.[1]

The conditions of perfect competition referred to on p. 49, have, on the whole, tended to prevail in the production of A goods. But deliberate attempts at the control of output by producers' agreements have recently been made in a large number of cases.

B. When much labour is embodied in the working up of raw materials into a finished or half-finished condition, the resulting commodities are apt to be somewhat specialized in character, differing in quality and detail of design according to the place in which the manufacturing process is carried out. These differences destroy the unity of the world market. English electrical apparatus designed for a certain purpose may be different in various particulars from German electrical apparatus designed for the same purpose. Consequently machinery for organizing a single world price for such apparatus cannot come into play. Each type of product has its own price. The difference between such prices is often greater than the qualitative differences of the products might be expected to justify. An organized market establishes an impersonal contact between those who have a demand for and those who have a supply of the commodity there dealt in. In the absence of such a market, the contacts are of a more personal kind, goodwill is established between buyer and seller, channels of trade become stereotyped, habits are formed and the substitution of German goods for similar English goods

[1] Quantitative restrictions on trade have modified this, and price differences for A goods have been maintained for periods of substantial length since the Second World War, particularly between hard and soft currency areas (see below, p. 104). It is noteworthy that in the progressive removal of restrictions priority has tended to be given to A goods, partly because producers in soft currency areas were put at a competitive disadvantage by the higher prices of raw materials temporarily prevalent.

can only be secured by a bigger price differential than that corresponding to the difference in the utility of the goods.

To this category of goods many services also belong. Insurance or the issue of securities ought, it might be thought, to be susceptible of international standardization. But many differences in the detail of national law and custom creep in, to distinguish the quality of the services offered at various commercial centres. In consequence of this firms can establish relations of goodwill with their clients, habits are formed and an international unity of market is not achieved.

C. Some goods and services are by their nature incapable of entering into international trade. Such are houses, fixed plant, railway services, public utility services, and domestic services; these cannot be moved from their location.

Retail goods must in general be regarded as amalgams of A (or B) and C goods. This fact has important implications, as will subsequently appear. The price of coal to the domestic consumer is, it is well known, very much higher than its price at the pit-head. The prices of all goods in the shop window stand well above the prices at which those goods are discharged from the factory. The difference is due to the many services which have to be performed in transporting the goods and making them available for the retail purchaser's selection. If the goods were to be exported, such services would be irrelevant. When the goods reach the shop window they must be regarded as embodying a purely domestic (C) element; they would only be capable of being exported at a value far below that which they are now expected to have attained; they have been metamorphosed from tradable into non-tradable goods.

There is no international price level for Class C goods. The price levels of these goods in different countries are related to each other only through the relation of each to the A and B goods.

We have then before us the following problems:

(i) What determines the international price level, that is, the common world price level of A goods?

(ii) What determines each national price level of C goods?

(iii) B goods stand in an intermediate position. There is some tendency towards a common international price level. But complete uniformity is seldom achieved and for long periods there may be considerable differences between the prices of similar B goods of different national origin.

The discussion of this chapter presupposes some common world monetary standard, such as gold. The complications which arise when various countries have independent standards must be postponed, until the monetary mechanism has been explored.

§ 2. The Price Level of International Goods.

The traditional treatment of monetary theory is not wholly satisfactory for the study of international trade. This treatment uses the concept of a general price level, which is the reciprocal of the value of gold. The general price level can thus be shown to depend on the demand and supply of gold, which in turn depends, when allowance has been made for its industrial uses, on the quantity of valuables it has to be exchanged against, on the rapidity with which it is turned over, on the extent to which substitutes for it are used (notes, cheques, etc.) and on its quantity. The equation embodying this truth, which is known as the quantity theory of money, may then be set out.

The validity of this theory cannot be shaken, but its employment is not of great service in the elucidation of the problem before us. If it is applied on a world scale, it determines, not the international price level, that is, the average of the prices of A goods which have a common international price, but the *general* world price level, which must include the prices of all valuables exchanged and, in particular, of samples of B and C goods from all nations. The quantity equation applied on a world scale does not bring out the relation of the international price level to the national price levels.

The international price level does depend partly on the relation of the quantity of gold and its efficiency in use to the

world output of goods.   But it also depends on the relation
of the demand and supply of world goods to the aggregate
demand and supply of all national (C) and quasi-national (B)
goods. It is sometimes rashly assumed that, if the production of
gold were sufficient to keep pace with the increase in the world
production of goods, the international price level would remain
steady.   But this would not occur if the value of international
goods happened to decline, as it probably will over a long
period, for reasons stated in Chapter III, § 4 and in § 4 below,
relatively to a sample of all national goods.   Even if the production of gold were sufficient to keep pace with the increased
world production of goods, the international price level would
probably fall. This, conjoined with a rise of other price
levels, might be accepted as a necessary evil, but its incidence
on the burden of international debts should be noticed.   Since
these can only be paid in international and quasi-international
(B) goods,[1] the burden of international debts, payable with
relatively depreciating assets, must increase, even if the general
value of the gold in which they are expressed were held stable.[2]

The unity of the international price level is disturbed by
transport costs and broken by tariffs.   In the case of A goods,
a traveller leaving a centre of output will ascend a slope of
rising prices until he reaches the watershed which bounds the
area supplied by a neighbouring centre.   The level at the
various centres is not necessarily the same.   The price at each
centre plus the cost of transport to the watershed dividing them,
must be the same.   If the gradient of the ground (i.e. the cost
of transport per mile) is the same on either side of the watershed, the price will be lower at whichever of the centres is
further from the watershed.   Generally prices will tend to be
low near the large centres of supply.   But quite small centres

[1] Also called above quasi-national goods. These terms are clearly
interchangeable.
[2] The *real* burden will not increase if the reason for the relative fall of
A goods is a relative increase of efficiency in producing them; but it will
increase in so far as the fall is due to the sluggishness of factors in transferring themselves to the production of goods for which there is a relative
rise in demand.

may reach very low levels if the gradient in the neighbourhood is steep. Small centres may also be found at very high levels. The demand may be thought of as being drained into the centres of supply, lakes whose sizes depend on the amount of the demand which they satisfy.

Tariffs are dams impeding the flow of demand outwards from a given area (but not impeding the flow, if there be one, in the contrary direction). If some of the demand flows out over the dam, the price inside will exceed that outside by the amount of the tariff. If, however, the tariff is completely obstructive, the price inside may stand anywhere between the price outside plus the tariff and the price outside. The price immediately inside the dam cannot fall below the price immediately outside it, for it does not obstruct the inward flow of demand.

§ 3. The Price Level of Quasi-International Goods.   A traveller exploring the price level of B goods finds somewhat different scenery. In the first place the ground is rougher, partly because tariffs are more numerous and higher, but also because the market is incompletely organized and the cost of salesmanship is heavier. Different prices for very similar goods may be found in close geographical proximity, if trade is running in old channels. The margin of a centre's market may not be the most distant part of it. One feature may strike him particularly. In the case of A goods he found that, as he approached a centre, prices fell to a minimum in its immediate vicinity. In the case of B goods he may find an opposite phenomenon—prices rising as he approaches the centre of supply. He is then in the presence of the notorious and unduly maligned practice of Dumping. The centre of supply will in this case prove to consist, not of a large number of producers operating in conditions of ideal competition, but of a single firm or group of firms able to exploit the market to the best of their advantage. They can charge a higher price near the centre of their area because that is most distant from the rival centres. In pure competition it is only to consumers in close proximity to the watershed that it is nearly a matter of indifference which centre they draw their supplies from; to those much nearer one centre than another it is a great advantage to draw from their own centre. The monopolist or quasi-monopolist exploits this advantage and extracts a higher price from his immediate neighbours than he gets from those on the periphery.

For this reason a country which exports more B goods than she imports is likely to have a higher general price level than the country which imports more B goods than she exports. For, since we may suppose such a country to import more A goods than she exports, the price level of the A goods will probably be higher than that of the country in the opposite position, to cover the higher cost of transport of the A goods; the price level of her B goods, on the other hand, will not be proportionately lower and may not be lower at all.

From the nature of the contours the traveller may get some glimpse of the future. If high and low priced B goods of similar quality are selling side by side, the high priced centre is only maintaining its position by a goodwill that is bound to wear down with time. The area controlled by the centre supplying the high priced B goods is probably subject to a long period recession.

Another rough generalization may be made about the B goods price level. In a period of falling world demand and a falling general price level, the production of goods will tend to be cut down. Suppose that there is no general fall in the reward to factors of production. In the case of A goods the law of increasing costs comes into play and the lower world prices are met by a restriction of production which reduces their real cost. B goods are more generally subject to the law of decreasing costs over a wide range on the productive side. A restriction of output may have no tendency to reduce real costs. It will therefore have to be pushed further if the new price is to cover the cost. If there is no reduction in rewards, the price of B goods will be sustained and the fall in demand will have to be met by a sufficient restriction of output. The

A industries will complain chiefly of over production and low prices in the slump, while the B industries will complain of excess capacity and unemployment; output will be more sharply restricted in the latter and the price level better sustained.

§ 4. The Price Levels of Domestic Goods.

It is now necessary to approach the problem of the relation of the national price levels of C goods to the international price level of A goods. The class of C goods as originally defined includes the fixed capital of the country. The following remarks do not apply to the price of existing capital equipment, but only to that of new equipment (of kinds that cannot be exported) as well as to all C services such as transportation, retailing, catering, public utility services, etc.

Any two countries will tend to have the same price of C goods if the three following conditions are fulfilled. If these conditions fail, the price level of C goods will be unequal in the two countries.

It should be remembered that the goods falling into this class differ according to the tastes and habits of different countries, and difficulties of detail arise in any attempt to measure the price levels against each other. This analysis only aims at a broad result.

(i) The ratio of the efficiency in producing C goods to that in producing A goods must be the same in the two countries.

(ii) The rewards to factors of production must either be the same in A industries as they are in C industries in each country, or the ratio of the rewards in A industries to those in C industries must be the same in both countries. (The former of these alternatives is a special case of the latter.)

(iii) The average excess of price over money cost, if any (this being due to monopolistic or quasi-monopolistic conditions among producers), in respect of C goods must bear the same relation to the excess of price over money cost, if any, in respect of A goods in both countries.

With regard to the first condition, it may be observed that

great differences between national levels of efficiency are usually due either to differences in natural resources or to difference in the degree to which scientific knowledge and capital have been applied to manufacturing processes. Both these differences affect the production of A and B goods. On the side of retailing, transport and domestic service it is doubtful if differences in efficiency occur on so great a scale. Since gold rewards are proportional to efficiency in the output of tradable goods, highly efficient countries may find the gold cost of providing their C services, in which proportional economies cannot be made, higher than that in the less efficient countries. It may be expected therefore, that the price level of C goods will be higher in the more efficient countries. Experience confirms this theoretic conclusion.

The cost of living is compounded of the prices of A, B and C goods. The efficient countries will therefore tend to have a high cost of living.

If the second condition is not fulfilled and rewards in the sheltered industries exceed those in the unsheltered industries by more in one country than another, the output of the sheltered industries will, *ceteris paribus*, be more highly priced in the former country.

The popular idea that in times of change there will be greater pressure to adjust rewards to factors in the unsheltered (A and B) industries than in the sheltered (C) industries is well founded. Whereas a period of slump involves some contraction in the demand for C goods and therefore some pressure to reduce rewards, a fall in the world price level of A and B goods may leave a country, whose rewards remain stationary, high and dry, in the sense that none of its A and B products could be marketed at all if costs had to be covered at the old level of rewards.

While the tendency to equality of the price levels of A goods and, within broader limits, of B goods in different countries is indisputable, it cannot be said that there is such a tendency in respect of goods in general. On the contrary, a general equality of prices in which C goods—and all retail goods have an important C element—are included would only be realized in special and unlikely circumstances.

If countries have, as has been assumed hitherto, a common monetary standard, such as gold, prices may be compared directly. If there is no common standard, prices in each country are expressed in terms of different national units and must be measured against those in other countries by reference to the rates at which the national currencies exchange with each other.

Whatever the rates of exchange ruling, the prices of A goods, so measured, will not vary outside the limits imposed by the costs of transport and tariffs.

If countries have no common monetary standard, fluctuations may occur in the rates at which their currencies exchange against each other. Some of these fluctuations may be caused by transient day-to-day conditions. An attempt has been made to distinguish such fluctuations from those due to the normal trend by reference to comparative national price levels. This attempt is known as the Theory of Purchasing Power Parity. It is asserted that the rate at which currencies exchange against each other should normally be that rate which causes each, when converted into the other, to purchase the same quantity of goods in the land of the currency into which it has been converted as it purchases at home. That the purchasing power may diverge within the limits imposed by the cost of transport and tariffs is recognized.

If attention is confined to A goods, it is clear that currencies converted at the ruling rates of exchange will purchase the same quantity of these, whatever the rate of exchange. For as quotations are telegraphed from centre to centre, each centre calculates the rate at which it will quote for A goods by taking the rates, at which the currencies of each centre exchange, into account. In each country A commodity prices are purely the effect of the foreign exchange rate and cannot be used to determine what that rate of exchange should normally be.

When C goods are taken into account the Theory of Purchasing Power Parity is no longer true. For C goods are not expected to have the same prices in different countries, except in the unusual case in which the three conditions referred to above are fulfilled.   If the degree of failure of actual conditions to correspond to those postulated were known and could be accurately measured, it would be possible to deduce the normal rate of foreign exchange from the actual price of C goods.   The normal rate of exchange must correspond to purchasing power parity after the failure of these conditions to be realized has been taken into account.   If a simultaneous shift occurs both in the normal rate of exchange and in the degree of failure of these conditions to be realized, whether the latter shift is necessarily cause and the former effect, or whether the rôles may be reversed, we are not yet in a position to consider.   We can only do so after a study of the monetary system.

§ 5. The Price Levels of Factors of Production.   Factors of production are like C goods in that there is no tendency towards a common international price level.   Uniformity of price level is brought about by the free flow of demand from a high to a low level and the flow of goods in the opposite direction.   Some of the factors are completely immobile, between nations, others have a very limited degree of mobility. Mines, land, railways, and fixed equipment cannot be moved at all.   There is some international flow of labour, but a very small one relatively to the large wage differences which exist. Migration is impeded by the cost of movement, by the many sacrifices which the severance of home ties and the abandonment of well-tried habits of life involve and, especially in recent times, by severe national restrictions on immigration.   The movement of scientific knowledge, business ability, and industrial skill is also extremely slow and sticky.   Free capital moves somewhat more easily.   Foreign investment in fixed interest securities is restricted by the possibility that the lending or borrowing country may depart from the gold standard, and by the investor's ignorance of the chances of default owing to political or economic disturbances in the borrowing country. Other forms of foreign investment are also restricted by the

investor's ignorance of the true prospect of the success of enterprises in distant lands. International movement of free capital on a large scale does nevertheless occur.

Classical writers made the immobility of factors of production the basis of the division between their treatment of national and that of international trade. Within the country it was assumed that rewards to factors in different employments might legitimately be regarded as tending to equality. As between different countries this is not even an approximation to the truth.[1] In a closed national system the proper distribution of productive resources among occupations is that which makes the output in all have equi-marginal utility. To secure equi-marginal utility of output in the world as a whole, the factors of production would have to be moved from one nation to another on a vast scale. The output of productive resources in the U.S.A. or England has exceeded and will long continue to exceed the output in Poland or India. To secure the best international division of labour with the existing distribution of population and skill, it is necessary to fall back on the principles already enunciated. Goods should be allowed to flow between countries so as to secure that the *ratios* of the output per head in different occupations should be approximately equal in all countries. The *absolute level* of output must remain different in different countries, so long as the factors of production cannot flow freely between them. The countries which have the higher absolute level are the more efficient countries.

Broadly, rewards to factors in each country are in proportion to their efficiency. The substantial truth as well as the limitations to this doctrine may be demonstrated by supposing the opposite. In what follows it is assumed that the relation of prices to costs in the world as a whole is such that productive resources in the world generally are in reasonably full employment. The opposite condition receives examination in a subsequent chapter (Ch. VII), but is not relevant to a consideration of the relative position of countries. First suppose

[1] Cf. ch. I, sec. 3.

rewards in a particular country to be low in relation to her efficiency. Rewards may be apparently but not really low in this sense. For instance, low wages per hour may so impair the health and efficiency of wage-earners, that a rise would increase output per unit of wage cost. To raise wages above such a level would be to make them lower "in relation to the efficiency of the country", and conversely. If rewards are low, the prices which a country can obtain by the sale of her A and B goods will then on the average exceed the rewards payable to her factors in respect of their productive services. But this is impossible. The price received for a commodity must be divided among factors of production. It follows that the sum total of rewards payable in respect of a representative parcel of her output cannot be less than the price obtainable for it.

A distinction may, however, be drawn between the relatively inflexible rewards to factors, whose rate is pre-determined by contract or agreement, and the adjustable item of profits. The sum total of inflexible rewards may be low in relation to the efficiency of a country, profits being correspondingly high. If this condition persists pressure may be brought to bear to raise the inflexible rewards. In accordance with the general theory of value, each factor will be rewarded in proportion to its own marginal net product. It should be observed in passing, however, that if one of the factors, such as labour, is not well organized to press its claim for a rise in reward when occasion offers, it may, in certain circumstances, continue for a long period to be paid a reward which is low in relation to the productive capacity of the country, it may continue so to say, to be "exploited"; the certain circumstances may be defined as those in which employers are in a quasi-monopolistic condition *vis-à-vis* labour. This, in its turn, may be explained as the condition, which is indeed the usual one in the absence of collective bargaining, in which a rise in the demand price of labour does not operate through an organized market, but is volunteered by an employer. An employer who offers such a rise has to pay more not only for the increment of labour he may wish to take on, but for all the labour he is already employing, and tends to make the marginal product of labour equal not to the wage he pays, but to the total increment of outlay in which the rise of wages required to attract the marginal increment of labour involves him.[1] Wages will then stand below the marginal net product of labour.

Secondly, suppose that rewards are high in relation to the efficiency of the country. At first sight this might also appear to be impossible since not more than the price obtained for the representative parcel of products can be paid out to factors. Inflexible rewards might indeed be high, profits in this case being squeezed. The two converse suppositions of low and high inflexible rewards do not, however, lead to similarly opposed results. If profits are high there is a tendency towards expansion of output, but this is ultimately limited by what is physically possible. The total output of a country cannot exceed the physical capacity of her productive resources. If profits are low, on the other hand, there is a persistent tendency towards contraction. The process of contraction does not meet with a physical obstacle analogous to that which opposes itself to a limitless expansion. As contraction proceeds, it may, if confined to one country, produce a new equilibrium. By restricting output a country tends to confine herself to the fields in which her comparative advantage is greatest. By limiting the scope of her activity, she raises her own efficiency per unit. Thus the sum total of all rewards cannot be high in relation to her efficiency in the output which she actually undertakes; but they may be high in relation to her efficiency in the broader sphere of what she could undertake, were rewards not so high. High rewards are secured at the cost of the partial unemployment of her productive resources. A further discussion of the relation of unemployment to foreign trade is found in Chs. VI and VII.

A country which relies chiefly on the production of B goods

---

[1] Cf. the analysis of the relation of cost of production to increment of receipts in the case of the quasi-monopolistic producer of goods in ch. III, pp. 50–51.

is in a rather worse position than one relying chiefly on A goods, when faced with the demand by factors for rewards in excess of what efficiency justifies.   The A goods country raises, at the cost of unemployment, the average productive efficiency of factors in the various fields of employment by the operation of the law of increasing productive costs in the production of A goods.[1]   But B goods are often not subject to this law over a wide range on the productive side.   The restriction of output may not raise the average efficiency on the productive side in respect of *each* of these goods.   If the production of the least profitable types is abandoned altogether, average efficiency may be somewhat higher in the remaining field than it was in the whole field before.   But in the types some output of which is still undertaken, there will probably be no gain of efficiency in production, the adjustment, if any, being made through the abandonment of the less accessible markets.   But as the foreign competitor approaches, the new frontier may soon become as hard to defend as the old one.   The higher reward is being paid in part out of a capital asset—goodwill.   As time passes, if there is no adjustment of productive efficiency to reward, or reward to productive efficiency, more and more goodwill may have to be sacrificed progressively, and, without any further widening of the gap between reward and efficiency, unemployment will grow.

To recapitulate, the sum total of all rewards must be proportional to the efficiency of a country in respect of the output which she undertakes.   The sum total of inflexible rewards may be low in relation to that efficiency, but this will be precisely offset by high profits.   The sum total of inflexible rewards may also be high in relation to that efficiency, if profits are correspondingly low; this condition is unstable, however, as output will tend to contract.   Finally, the sum total of all rewards may be high in relation to the efficiency of a country in respect of her potential output; in this case there will be unemployment.

[1] This means the real costs *decrease* and productive efficiency increases when production is restricted.

6

The foregoing analysis did not take account of the fact that not all output is marketed at world prices. That level of rewards may be regarded as neither high nor low in relation to her efficiency which enables a country to sell, at a normal rate of profit, enough to give employment to all productive resources *other than* those engaged in C industries. C goods may be divided into two classes, consumable C goods (and services) and immovable capital goods. What determines the proportion of total resources devoted to providing consumable C goods (and services) may be stated fairly simply. Since the total income is equal to the sum of rewards to all factors, the proportion of resources devoted to the production of C consumables is equal to the proportion of total income expended upon them. (This statement has to be modified if part of income is derived from foreign investments or foreign gifts; more will be said of this later.) The proportion of productive resources devoted to the output of fixed capital is, in equilibrium, determined by the rate of saving of the community and the technique of industry. At any given time there is therefore a definite proportion of total productive resources, which, if the system is in equilibrium, are devoted to C output. The level of rewards proper to a country may therefore be defined as that which enables such a quantity of goods to be marketed at world prices with a normal rate of profit, that, if the employment so given is added to employment given by C industries when in their normal relation to the A and B industries, the productive resources of the country are in reasonably full employment. If inflexible rewards are higher than this there will be unemployment, if lower, inflated profits.

There is much popular misconception regarding the detriment to the home country that is due to the prevalence of low wage rates elsewhere. If many countries are less efficient than the home country, wages must necessarily be lower in them; the low wage is offset by low efficiency. Of course the low wage may also be due to the ability of the other factors to secure a larger share of the product; in this case the low wage is offset by high profits or rents. Low wages in foreign countries are decried on the ground that they give those countries an unfair competitive advantage; this attitude is highly confused. A foreign country's power as a competitor depends on the volume and nature of her production; the payment of low wages will not allow her to force production above the level determined by the numbers and skill of her people. She cannot sell more than she can produce. We are benefited if the foreign country can maintain production at a high level, unless she happens to specialize in the goods which we export.[1] In this one case we are injured by her prosperity and would gain if her output declined. To complain of her low wages means nothing unless it means that we should like her to put her wages so high as to restrict her output and create unemployment in her own land; and this is more than we can in fairness expect.

Low wages abroad may be condemned for keeping the health and efficiency of workpeople there at a low level and so reducing the real wealth of the foreign country. In accordance with the second principle of Chapter II, anything which reduces the real wealth of the outer world is likely to reduce the gain accruing to this country from foreign trade. But this is not the score on which low wages abroad are usually decried. The level of wages in foreign countries has no direct relevance to the proper level of wages at home.

Changes in the general world level of A and B prices are clearly relevant; but it is important to guard against the fallacy of using the low costs or prices elsewhere *of particular commodities* as evidence that wages at home are too high. Rewards to factors are proportional to the general level of a country's efficiency. It does not follow that there is any meaning in saying that rewards in any particular trade are or should be proportional to the country's efficiency in that trade. Efficiency, i.e. the value of output per unit of factor employed in the production of a particular commodity, depends on how much output of the commodity is undertaken by the country. To make rewards proportional to the efficiency of factors

[1] Cf. ch. II, p. 37.

producing a particular commodity in a country, when engaged in satisfying all and no more than that country's own needs for this commodity, would be equivalent to dispensing with all foreign trade. If it is said that rewards to factors producing a commodity are or should be proportional to their efficiency in producing that amount of the commodity which the country actually produces, the proposition is true but states nothing. For how much will she produce? That amount which, given the rewards to factors *and* their efficiency, she can market at home or abroad. Of the three variables, efficiency, rate of reward, and the amount of production of the particular commodity, if two are known the other can be determined. But if only one is known, efficiency, the other two cannot be deduced from that.

§ 6. **Law of Comparative Costs and the Price Mechanism.** The exposition of the Law of Comparative Costs (Ch. II) showed the circumstances in which a gain from trade is possible; it envisaged the direct exchange of two commodities. Between countries where private enterprise is prevalent, such a direct exchange is only undertaken exceptionally ("Barter Agreements"). When completely centralist economies, however, enter into trade the phenomenon may be more frequent.

We are now in a position to explain how the abstract principle embodied in the Law of Comparative Costs works out when trade is conducted through private channels. A producer or merchant will sell abroad if he can get a remunerative price; he pays no attention to the nature or price of the commodity, whatever it may be, which is bought abroad by his fellow countrymen in the import business; that is no concern of his.

In the foregoing section it was stated that in each country factor rewards expressed in gold (or in national currencies converted at ruling rates of exchange) tend to be proportional to the efficiencies of those factors in their own country. This now requires more precise definition. For this purpose reference may be made to Table XVI (p. 35 above). We

cannot infer from this Table which of the commodities will be
imported by the home country. For instance A might be so
important a commodity, its cost gradients so low and the
demand for it so expansible in the home country in response
to a lower price, that the rest of the world could obtain all they
required of the commodities B, C, D, E and F from the home
country by exporting to it A only. Let us suppose that the
commodities are better balanced than that, and that the home
country imports A, B and C, sending out in exchange E and
F. In consequence of this, the price ratios of each pair of
those five commodities will move towards equality in the two
countries.

Let us now suppose that, when so much of commodities A,
B and C are imported and when so much of E and F are
exported as to render the price ratios between all five commodities at home equal to those abroad, trade balances. If
this is the case, then for sustaining the balance there must be
no trade either way in D; if D were exported, this would give
the home country a favourable balance, and conversely.

Returning now to the point of view of the private trader,
it is necessary, if D is to move neither way in trade, that its
quoted price abroad should be roughly equal (subject, as
always, to transport costs) to its price at home. Now we
learn from Table XVI that, prior to trade, D costs x to produce
at home and $3y$ to produce abroad. Accordingly, if D is not
to enter into trade, it is necessary that the price of x should be
three times the price of y. This gives the quoted price of D
at home as $1 \times 3 \ (=3)$ and that abroad as $3 \times 1 \ (=3)$.

The symbol x was used throughout Ch. II to stand for a
unit of productive resources. Nothing was said about what
kind of resources these were; it was also explained that x
might be thought of in terms of labour days, £s sterling, baskets
full of commodities, etc. We might take x to mean *among
other things* the price that had to be paid, prior to trade, to one
particular kind of labour day, say a transport-labour-day.
More generally x would then stand for any group of factors
of production that had the same value, prior to trade, as a

transport labour day. When it is stated in Table XVI that a unit of A requires the same amount of x for its production as a unit of D, this does not imply that A uses the same factors of production as D, but only that the group of factors that a unit of A does require has the same value in the home country as the group that D requires.

Now we pass to abroad. In the strict analysis of Ch. II we refused to admit that there was any need to suppose the same factors were used at home and abroad; all the work at home might be done by robots, abroad by human beings. But in the looser discussion of the present chapter we have been comparing rewards to the same factors in different countries. It may be that there is no factor abroad that can be said to be exactly the same as a home-country transport-labour-day; it may be that all foreign labour has quite a different working capacity. For the purpose of this chapter, where we are comparing rewards in different countries, we may assume that there is a foreign transport-labour-day equivalent to the domestic transport-labour-day. y will then stand for the price of a foreign transport-labour-day, or any group of factors that has the same price in total abroad as that of one transport-labour-day. The various possible compositions of x will not necessarily be the same as those of y. Thus at home the equivalent in value of one transport-labour-day might be half a transport-labour-day plus 50 acres, while abroad it might be half a transport-labour-day plus 100 acres, the relative valuation of land and labour being different in the two regions. For the rough purposes of this chapter, let us take x to stand simply for the wage of a day's labour at home (or for any group of factors having the same price in total as a labour day), and y for the wage of a day's labour (or similar factors) abroad.

If the price quotation of D is to be such that it is not profitable to trade it either way, wages must be three times as high at home as abroad. Thus the commodity D may be used as a yardstick for giving precise meaning to the proposition that wages (and other factor rewards) should be proportional to the country's comparative efficiency *on average*.

The word "average" is defined in the following sentence. Let there be a commodity (viz D of the last paragraph) the home country's comparative efficiency in producing which is such that, if she exports all commodities in which she has a greater initial comparative efficiency and imports all commodities in which she has a less initial comparative efficiency (in amounts sufficient to bring all the price ratios between members of those two groups to equality), trade balances; the country's comparative efficiency in producing such a commodity is defined as her *average* comparative efficiency. If rewards to factors are proportional to that average efficiency, then it will not be profitable to trade in this borderline commodity either way; its quoted price will be the same at home and abroad.

It is the tendency of rewards to factors to be proportional to average efficiency in this sense that *transmutes the law of comparatives costs into a law of relative prices operating upon private traders*. The exporter or importer knows nothing about comparative costs; all he knows are the quoted prices at home and abroad. If rewards to factors are correctly adjusted, trade will move on the lines indicated by the law of comparative costs.

Thus if, in our example, the price of any group of factors represented by $1x$ is 3 and the price of any group of factors represented by $1y$ is 1, A, B, and C will be priced respectively, prior to trade, at 1×3 ($=3$), 1×3 ($=3$) and 1×3 ($=3$) at home, while abroad they will be priced at 1×1 ($=1$), 2×1 ($=2$), and $2 \cdot 5 \times 1$ ($=2 \cdot 5$); in all these cases the foreign prices are lower. E and F will be priced at 1×3 ($=3$) and 1×3 ($=3$) at home and at 5×1 ($=5$) and 10×1 ($=10$) abroad; here the home prices are lower.

Now suppose that matters have not worked out so happily and that rewards (other than profit) in the home country are *low* by the aforementioned criterion—say $2\frac{1}{2}$ per unit of x. The result may be that the cost (including a normal profit) of commodity D falls below its price abroad by enough to cover transport costs. Thus the cost of D will be $1 \times 2\frac{1}{2}$ ($=2\frac{1}{2}$)

compared with the foreign price of 3. It does not follow that D will be exported. For with rewards established in the country generally below the appropriate level, higher profit will be earned on all goods. If we suppose that, when rewards are at an appropriate level, the economy is fully employed in producing commodities E and F for export and for the home market, in producing such amounts of A, B and C as are needed to supplement its imports and in producing appropriate amounts of non-tradable goods (p. 68 above), all at an adequate level of profit, then, if rewards are below the appropriate level, all this activity can be carried on at an enhanced profit. Entrepreneurs will find enough to produce at an enhanced profit to employ all the factors in the country. In these conditions there will be no motive for anyone to explore the possibility of exporting D, even although some profit could be made on that also. When the whole economy is fully employed at an enhanced level of profit, there is no point in directing resources to the additional production of D at a merely normal level of profit. If D is not due for export under the law of comparative costs, it will not be exported even if rewards to factors are depressed below the appropriate level.

Next suppose that rewards are *above* the appropriate level. This may render the export of E an unprofitable proposition, reduce the amount of F that can profitably be exported, raise the quantitites of A, B and C that can profitably be imported, and perhaps make D a profitable import. This will lead to the under-employment of the factors in the home country. There will be less work to be done at home throughout the range of these six commodities and, because the flow of income at home will be depresed by consequence, less demand for and work to be done on non-tradable goods also. This situation can only be fully explored when we have taken certain other matters relevant to the full employment problem into account, as we shall do in Chapters VI and VII.

§ **7. Summary.** The conclusions of this chapter may be summarized:

(i) For A goods there are common world prices. The price of each A commodity in one place will not differ from its price in another by more than the cost of transporting it between them, plus the monetary equivalent of any impediment to trade, such as a tariff, dividing them.

(ii) The prices of B goods also tend towards a common level. But the forces operating to bring about this result have to overcome greater friction than in the case of A goods; moreover B goods of the same description produced in different centres are apt to differ to some extent in kind.

(iii) There is no world price level for C goods. The national price levels are only related through the relation of each to the price levels of the other classes. There are conditions in which national price levels for C goods will be equal, but these are not likely to be realized. Consumable C goods and all retail goods are likely to be more expensive in more efficient countries.

(iv) There is no world price for factors of production. Each national price level is proportional to the efficiency of the factors in making A and B commodities.

(v) It is through the tendency of rewards to factors to be fixed at levels proportional to their efficiencies in their own countries that the law of comparative costs is translated into a law of relative prices actuating private traders.

(vi) If rewards to factors are fixed below the appropriate level, profits will be abnormally high, but the operation of the law of comparative costs will not be distorted. If rewards are fixed above the appropriate level, this will tend to cause unemployment. This will be further discussed in Chapters VI and VII.

CHAPTER V

FOREIGN EXCHANGE

§ **1. The Balance of Payments (introductory).** If an imaginary boundary line were drawn around any area of the world's surface, an inventory could be made of all the payments moving over the line, some proceeding outwards, others inwards. These payments could be divided into those arising out of purchases, loans and gifts. Money may be paid in exchange for goods and services, it may be lent or repaid, or it may be given. This seems to be an exhaustive classification of the reasons for which money may pass from the pockets of residents on one side of the line to those of residents on the other side. It is not, however, quite all the money that passes over, for residents themselves may move out or in, taking money with them.

Payments out may thus be classified according to the purposes for which they are made as follows:

(i) Importation of goods and services.
(ii) (*a*) Loans to the outer world.
    (*b*) Repayment of loans previously made by the outer world to the area.
(iii) Gifts, including indemnity payments, made to the outer world.
(iv) (*a*) Expenditure of tourists travelling in the outer world.
    (*b*) Money taken by emigrants leaving the area for the outer world.

The first of these (i) may be further subdivided:

(*a*) "Visible" import of commodities.
(*b*) Payments made for the use of such foreign services as insurance, brokerage, etc.
(*c*) Interest and profit on foreign capital invested in the area.

Payments coming into the area may be classified in a similar way.[1] Thus each division and subdivision involves or may involve both payments out and in. It is important to bear in mind on which side of the balance-sheet each item comes. The importation of goods, the income derived from investments made by foreigners in the country, loans to foreigners and the expenditure of nationals travelling abroad, for instance, all come on the same side. The exportation of goods, the income from foreign investments, foreign loans to the area, the expenditure of foreign tourists in the area all come on the other side.

Payments are often divided into those arising from "visible" and those from "invisible" items. The former class includes only the division (i) (*a*) above. All other items are invisible.[2]

Payments in and payments out may be cancelled against each other and the difference is the net balance of payments. If the payments in exceed the payments out, the balance is called positive, active or favourable. If the imaginary boundary line happens to be a national frontier, the money in use within will probably not have currency outside and the payment will have to be mediated by a "foreign exchange"

[1] Some authorities, such as the U.K. Board of Trade, publish figures for imports including freight charges ("c.i.f.") and for exports excluding them ("f.o.b."). If this is done, there should appear under payments *in* (*ib*) "earnings of home country's shipping companies"; no corresponding figure will appear for payments *out* to foreign shipping companies, as these are already included in the figure for imports. Other authorities, including the U.K. Central Statistical Office, give both imports and exports free of freight; if this is done, the shipping figure under payments *in* (*ib*) must be modified to "payments by *foreigners* to home country's shipping companies" and another item under payments *out* (*ib*) must appear, viz. "payments to foreign shipping companies".

[2] But there is an alternative and important use of the expression "visible balance", namely for the unadjusted trade balance, when imports are valued c.i.f. and exports f.o.b. In relation to the British balance, the term "visible" is normally used in this sense. This "visible" balance is less favourable to Britain than her balance of payments on account of commodities only, because it includes the debits arising on shipping account but not the credits, and also because it debits against Britain payments made by British importers to British shipping companies.

transaction, by which one national money is converted into another. These transactions can, however, only cover the payments which may be cancelled against each other; the net balance, active or passive, cannot be met in this way; local money can only be exchanged against foreign money in so far as there is a counterbalancing offer of foreign money to meet the offer of local money. If there is an unfavourable balance the excess of local money offered may be met by the offer of foreign money on short loan. But if we include short loans in estimating the balance and there remains a net deficit there is no means of covering it by a foreign exchange operation. If a gold, or silver, standard prevails within and without, gold or silver, may be exported or imported to cover the net balance. From this it may be deduced that when all items as well as short loans are included in computing the balance, the net excess of deficit must be equal to the quantity of the standard metal imported or exported. If trade in the precious metals be included in computing the balance, there can be no excess or deficit. Payments out must be exactly equal to payments in. If the country is not on a gold (or silver) standard foreign trade in these metals should be reckoned along with that in other commodities, and, as in the other case, there must be an exact balance of payments in and out. This is a principle of cardinal importance in the subject and failure to appreciate it leads to much confusion of thought in popular discussion.

§ 2. The Gold Standard and Gold Points. In the Foreign Exchange market those who, having the currency of one country, desire to acquire that of another, meet those who having the currency of the other desire to acquire that of the one. It may be well first to consider how this market works when a gold standard is in operation. Most countries were on a gold (or silver) standard before 1914 and for periods between the two world wars. Since the second war the trend has been towards a closer approximation to gold standard mechanisms than obtained immediately before it.

A gold standard implies that the value of the currency is

fixed in terms of gold. Reference to the official gold value of a unit of currency, a pound, a dollar, a franc, etc., determines the "par" of exchange. When the exchange is at par, a unit of one currency exchanges for units of another equal to the same amount of gold at the official valuations. For a gold standard to be effective the central monetary authority, the Central Bank or Treasury, must be willing to give in exchange for units of currency the amount of gold prescribed in the official valuation. Thus the holder of a currency in a country on an effective gold standard has always two possible methods of making a foreign payment: he may purchase the foreign currency in the foreign exchange market or he may acquire gold in exchange for currency from the central authority and remit it. The rate of exchange quoted in the market depends on the balance of supply and demand. If the demand for foreign currency is strong its value expressed in the market quotation tends to rise; if the demand for the home currency is strong the value of the home currency tends to rise.

The language of the foreign exchange market is rather confusing. If the conventional method of quoting a rate of exchange is the number of units of foreign currency which may be obtained for a unit of the home currency (as in the British market so many dollars, francs, etc., to the pound), the rate for these currencies is said to rise, if a greater number can be obtained for one pound, that is, if the exchange value of the foreign currency falls. If on the other hand the conventional method of quoting is the number of pounds, shillings, and pence required to obtain a foreign unit (e.g. so many pence to the rupee), a rise in the rate means the same as a rise in the value of the currency quoted. To avoid confusion, the rise of a currency is always used, in what follows, to mean a rise in its value, irrespective of the conventional method of quotation.

The alternative means of making payment, the remission of gold, sets a limit to the fluctuation of foreign exchange rates. By the remission of gold the currency of a foreign gold standard country may always be obtained at par. But the remission of gold has a cost, the principal elements in which are the cost of transport, insurance and interest during the period of transit. If a would-be purchaser of foreign currency is to use the foreign exchange method he must be able to get it, at worst, at a cost equal to its par value plus the cost of remitting gold; otherwise he will use the other method and remit gold. Private traders do not normally remit gold; this is done by arbitrage dealers who simultaneously buy gold at home with the local currency and sell forward for local currency the foreign currency that they expect to acquire in the foreign country when they have remitted the gold there. The quotation which makes the foreign exchange method equal in cost to the gold export method is called the gold export point and is the highest point to which the foreign exchange quotation of the foreign currency can rise while the gold standard is in operation in both countries. The quotation which makes the cost of the foreign exchange method for the foreigner to acquire the home currency equal to the cost of sending gold to the home country is called the gold import point and is the highest point to which the foreign exchange quotation of the home currency can rise.

It is not to be expected that the spontaneous flow of payments in and out arising out of normal transactions will balance day by day. On days when there is a strong spontaneous outward flow, foreign currency will become more expensive. This is a balancing factor. Banks and other firms which normally have balances in more than one centre can make the payments they need to make in any centre on a particular day out of the available balance in that centre, which is allowed to run down. They can thus, within limits, choose the time at which they convert one currency into another. The rise in the quotation of the foreign currency will lead them to postpone purchase if a relapse is expected at a later date. Foreign firms may also take advantage of the low price of the home currency to purchase it in advance of need. Thus if the spontaneous streams of payment are unequal, the movement in the quotation will thin one and supplement the other, tending to make them equal.[1]　Speculation may also be a balancing element.　If the fall in a quotation induces the expectation of a subsequent rise, the cheap currency will be bought to be resold at a profit at a later date.　If the spontaneous flow of the demand for the home currency is sufficiently weak, its quotation may fall to the gold export point.　The Central Bank must provide the gold or foreign exchange required to cover the deficiency, in exchange for units of currency, out of its reserve.　Its reserve of foreign exchange may consist of deposits in foreign banks, actual foreign currency, foreign Treasury Bills, or bills drawn on foreign firms.

Those desiring to purchase foreign currency will be equally well satisfied if the Bank provides them with gold or with foreign exchange in exchange for their own currency at a rate not higher than the gold export point.　The gold standard will be maintained if, as soon as the exchange quotation reaches the gold export point, the Bank sells a sufficient quantity of gold or foreign exchange, to prevent its quotation rising above that point.　To be able to do this the Bank must hold reserves of gold and/or foreign exchange.

If the Bank is legally obliged to offer gold in exchange for currency at par, the country is said to be on a gold standard. If it is only obliged to offer the currency of or bills on a foreign gold standard country at the gold export point, the country is said to be on a Gold Exchange standard.　Even if the Bank is legally obliged to offer gold it may in fact offer foreign exchange. Provided that the would-be purchaser can get foreign currency from the central bank at a rate not higher than the gold export point, its quotation in the open market cannot rise above the gold export point.　Individuals are concerned to get what they want at a rate not higher than this; it is indifferent to them whether they get gold at par or foreign exchange at the gold export point.

The central bank of a gold country is usually obliged by law to keep a certain reserve of gold.　But it may keep the reserves,

[1] For the operation of the flow of bills of exchange as a balancing element, see below, pp. 83–87.

which it actually intends to use to meet a foreign exchange demand, in the form of foreign exchange. Many central banks keep part of the reserves they hold in excess of legal requirements in this form. In some countries the law allows a part of the legal requirement also to be held in this form.

In order that the gold import point may also be effective, the central monetary authority, now usually the Central Bank, has the more welcome obligation to issue domestic currency in exchange for gold. This, however, is not always done at par. When the currency takes the form of gold coins the appropriate central authority to issue them is the Mint, which may wish to make a charge for coinage. Between 1666 and 1914 the English Mint made no such charge; it was, however, unwilling to issue coin on demand, but only after a period allowing time for the process of minting. The Bank of England was willing to issue coins on demand in return for a payment equivalent to interest on the process period, which was ultimately reduced to $1\frac{1}{2}$d. on £3 17s. $10\frac{1}{2}$d. (=1 oz. 22 carat gold). Thus the difference between the gold export and import points was not equal to twice the cost of remitting the gold between London and the foreign centre, but twice that cost plus $1\frac{1}{2}$d. an oz.

By widening the margin between its buying and selling price the Bank could widen the margin between the gold points. In his *Treatise on Money* [1] Lord Keynes gave reasons for thinking as large a margin as 2 per cent desirable. Such an arrangement would not be inconsistent with a gold standard. The natural course of events, on the other hand, is tending to reduce the margin between gold points due to the cost of remission.[2]

If the central bank is not obliged and does not, in fact, undertake [3] to buy and sell gold or foreign exchange in

[1] Op. cit., Vol. II, p. 325.
[2] Einzig, *International Gold Standard Movements*, ch. 9.
[3] The Secretary of State for India and the Government of India did between them in fact undertake to buy and sell sterling exchange for rupees at fixed rates between 1900 and 1914, though not legally obliged to do so. India was thus effectively on a Gold Exchange standard in that period. India is now on a Sterling Exchange standard.

exchange for the local currency at fixed rates, there is no limit to possible fluctuations of foreign exchange rates in the open market. The rates may then move freely under the influence of supply and demand. The probable course of foreign exchange in these circumstances must be studied in relation to the influences affecting supply and demand.

§ 3. Bills and the Bank Rate.

Reference has been made to foreign bills of exchange. In the nineteenth century these were the principal means by which foreign payments were effected. An Englishman wishing to make a payment in Paris would authorize the French firm to draw a bill on him, while a Frenchman wishing to make a payment in London would purchase such a bill. The bills might be payable on sight or after the lapse of ninety days. The quotations of the foreign exchange markets referred to the rates at which such bills could be bought and sold. The use of the telegraph and cable in due course facilitated the more direct bartering of bank deposits in different countries against each other by means of a telegraphic transfer ("T.T."), and the quotation for a bill came, in most cases, to be calculated from the T.T. quotation.

If someone in London has to make a payment in New York he may authorize the payee to draw a bill on him expressed in sterling payable at sight or with ninety days to run. The authorization is confirmed by his bank or accepting house, acting through its agent in New York. The drawer of the bill may sell it at once to his banker in New York for dollars. The present dollar value of a ninety-day bill is computed by subtracting interest for ninety days at the market rate current in London, which gives its present sterling value, and translating that into dollars at the current rate of exchange. The New York banker may then remit it to London to have it accepted by the bank or accepting house, referred to above, on behalf of the drawee. When this has been done, the bill is a liability both of the drawer and the firm which accepts it. It may then be discounted in London, and the American banker can buy dollars with the proceeds by cable. The discount house or

7

bank which discounts the bill in London is paid off by the acceptor when the bill matures. The creditor (drawer) thus receives his money approximately ninety days before the debtor (drawee) has to pay.

The flow of bills presented for discount at a financial centre is not determined solely by the flow of trade. A bill that has been drawn need not be discounted at once; it need not be discounted at the centre on which it is drawn; and an exporter may decide, on advice, that he will not finance his trade by a bill at all; he may, for instance, get an overdraft at his bank at home instead. Thus the flow of bills may be reduced in these three ways without there having been any change in the pattern of trade; or it may be increased.

There are two principal influences, other than the flow of trade (or investment), on the size of the flow of bills. If the exchange quotation of the currency of the country which has to make payment is low, particularly if it is near its lowest point, it may be better business for the holder or would-be drawer of a bill to wait awhile. If one discounts the bill at once, one has to pass the funds received through the foreign exchange market at a moment when the quotation of the paying country's currency is at its lowest. If one waits, it cannot fall much more, but during ninety days it may rise substantially; why cash in at the lowest point?

This influence of the exchange quotation on the flow of bills is a particular instance of the broader principle stated in the last section that the fall in the quotation of a currency may lead to a deferment by bankers and others of their intended sales of that currency until a more propitious moment. It should be noticed that this influence tends to even out the country's balance of payments. If a quotation is weak, that is because for the time being the supply of the currency is running ahead of the demand for it; but the fall in the quotation brings about a corrective influence, by thinning out the supply (and increasing the demand). The foreign exchange market is the most notable case where responsiveness to small price changes in the quest for gain exerts a stabilizing influence.

This presupposes that there is complete confidence in the future of the currency and no suspicion that there is any chance whatever of its being allowed to fall below the lower official point in the next ninety days. Any suspicion of devaluation brings about speculation which is the reverse of stabilizing.

When the exchange weakens, the central bank of the country must have some anxiety, for if it touches the lowest point the bank will have to meet any deficiency in the total payments out of its reserves.[1] The arbitrage dealers will at once sell foreign currency while at the same time presenting domestic currency for encashment into gold to be remitted to the foreign centre where they will acquire foreign currency at par to reimburse themselves for their previous sale of it in the foreign exchange market. This brings us to the second influence on the flow of bills.

The central bank can raise short-term interest rates at home by open market operations, supplemented, if necessary, by a rise in its official rate of discount. This may be expected to effect a strong reduction in the flow of bills, under all the three heads mentioned on p. 84. A rise in interest rates will not, however, have much effect if the foreign exchange quotation of the country's currency is initially high. In that case a foreigner holding a bill due in ninety days would be well advised to discount it at once, since it would be wiser to accept the high rate of discount than the risk that the currency in which payment is due will drop substantially in the course of ninety days. But if the quotation is near the bottom point, when the rise in interest rates occurs, then the curative effect of the rise is sure. By this method, when the overall balance is tending to be unfavourable, the country is able to cut down on an important debit item (short-term lending) and possibly to expand a credit item (short-term borrowing). This tends to bring the total balance to equality. When the overall

[1] The central banking system (Federal Reserve System) of the U.S. is probably the only one that has for several decades been aloof from anxiety on this account (except possibly in 1933), owing to the very large size of the U.S. gold reserve in relation to possible calls upon it.

balance is tending to be favourable, it should carry out the same process in reverse by reducing its interest rate.

With these two stabilizing weapons, fluctuations of the exchange quotation and movements in the interest rate on bills, it has been possible to reduce gold payments to a minimum whenever confidence in the future has been secure. It must be noticed that the curative effects of these movements have depended absolutely on there being a rigidly-fixed lower limit for the quotation, which could be implicitly relied on as unalterable.

In the twentieth century there has been a distinct trend in international, as well as in domestic, trade away from reliance on short-term accommodation. Firms have tended to have cash balances during the seasons of the year when receipts are in excess, and to draw them down in the spending seasons, rather than to be in near balance in the receiving seasons and run into the red, whether by overdraft or discount of bills, in the spending seasons. We need not speculate on whether that is due to firms being stronger financially than they were before, or less progressive and expansive, or less attentive to the pence.

In the British case there has been a special factor at work recently. Britain ran up heavy debts during the second war and, at the end of it, foreign central banks and other banks and firms found themselves with much unused sterling on hand. When these wanted accommodation or had to meet demands of clients, instead of coming to the London market with bills to discount, they could draw down their "sterling balances".

While this seems to reverse the situation for London, or for any other financial centre affected by the general trend towards replacing overdrafts by credit balances, the two movements described above (viz. in foreign exchange quotations and in short interest rates) should have the same influence on net international lending as before. For instance, the sterling balances are usually invested in Treasury Bills, rates on which move with, and indeed dominate, the short-term rates in the London market. A rise in the yield should tend to make banks

or traders defer intended sales or expedite intended purchases of sterling or even switch idle funds temporarily into
sterling.

Unfortunately there has not yet (1956) been much opportunity to test these great historic stabilizers in the new situation.
For there has not been that absolute confidence in the durability of the lower official point that is essential. The slightest
rumour of devaluation makes the stabilizers altogether
inoperative.

There have, however, been occasional instances of their
effective working. When in February 1955 there was a
temporary phase of confidence in sterling, the rise of the Bank
Rate had its traditional effect. Still more marked has been
the effect of high interest rates in Germany in 1956 in expediting
payments to that country.

§ **4. Forward Foreign Exchange.**   Something must also be said
of forward dealing.   If a currency becomes cheap, those who
have payments to make in the future may desire to take
advantage of the present rate without actually spending the
money required to make the payment in advance; they may
desire to secure themselves against future fluctuation, which is,
of course, highly important in the case of payments to and
from a country not on a stable standard.   The purchase of
forward foreign currency consists of a promise to pay home
currency for it at a specified future date at a rate agreed on
now.   The rate agreed on may differ from the rate at which
foreign currency can be purchased now (the "spot" rate).
What determines the difference?   Dealers in forward exchange
have to satisfy the demands of their clients; they undertake to
deliver the foreign currency at a specified future time at a rate
to be fixed now; they may be quite unwilling to speculate
at a client's behest on the foreign currency not becoming
dearer in the interval; consequently they must cover themselves
by purchasing the foreign money at once; this they invariably
do.   In doing so they have transferred their liquid funds from
one centre to another on the strength of a contract which

enables them to bring those funds home again at the rate agreed on.

The advantage or disadvantage of having their funds for a time at the foreign centre depends on the rate of interest which they can earn there compared with the rate of interest which they can earn at home. If the rate is higher abroad, it is an advantage, for which they are prepared to pay by selling forward currency below the spot rate. The forward deal enables them to earn the higher rate abroad without running the risk of the exchange moving against them before they bring their funds back. The forward dealers therefore tend to be willing to sell forward currency at a discount compared with spot by an amount equal, after deducting a commission for themselves, to the excess of what they can earn in the short market of the foreign country over what they could earn in the short market of the home country during the period of contract. If the rate is lower abroad, the forward rate exceeds the spot rate by the excess of what they could have earned in the home market over what they can earn in the foreign market plus a commission for themselves.

Actually dealers are both buying and selling foreign currencies forward, and their contracts made in the course of a day may cancel each other out. But every one must be covered when it is made, to avoid risk; if there is an equal balance at the end of the day the discount on forward sales cancels the premium on forward purchases (or vice versa) and the dealer's net profit is equal to the sum of the commissions on both.

If there is a lack of confidence in the future of a currency, those who wish to sell it forward will exceed those who wish to purchase it forward. The spot sales of forward dealers covering themselves will exceed spot purchases, and the opinion about the future of the currency is thus reflected in a present excess of supply over demand and a weakening in its spot quotation. This shadow, which the future casts before it, is particularly important in the case of currencies the exchange in which is not stabilized.

It is the difference between gold export and import points

that allows short rates of interest to be at a different level in centres on the same standard.

If the rate in London is lower than the rate in New York, why should not an American who has English connexions draw a bill on his agent in London, get it accepted and discounted there and acquire funds at the low rate for some purely domestic purpose? If such operations could be carried out on a sufficiently large scale the English rate would be forced up to the American level. But they cannot be. For the spot sterling quotation may rise in the interval and, when the American comes to acquire sterling to honour his bill, he may have to pay a larger number of dollars per pound than he acquired at the outset when he discounted the bill in London and sold the proceeds for dollars. If the maximum possible fluctuation is ·5 per cent, which represents a loss on a ninety-day bill of 2 per cent per annum, the rate in London would have to be more than 2 per cent lower than in New York to cover the risk of such a fluctuation. May not the American safeguard himself by purchasing forward sterling at the outset, that is, at the same moment that he sells spot sterling? No, because if the London rate of discount is below the American rate the forward price of sterling will exceed the spot price by precisely the amount which the American hopes to gain by borrowing money at the cheaper centre. The larger the gap between the gold points, the greater the possible divergence of interest rates between two centres with close commercial connexions. When the difference between rates is larger than that which the margin between gold points ought to allow, that must either be due to a lack of confidence in the stability of the currency in the high rate centre or because the firms in the high rate centre have not sufficient connexions with accepting and discount houses in the low rate centre to enable them to borrow there on a sufficiently large scale to produce an equalizing effect on the rates.

§ 5. Foreign Exchange in the Absence of a Gold Standard.   If the country is not on the gold standard, the Foreign Exchange method is the only method of making a foreign payment, and the rates move freely under the influence of supply and demand. Like other prices, they must make supply equal to demand. It does not follow that the supply and demand arising out of payments due in respect of normal transactions must balance from day to day, for when there is no par of exchange, speculative operations play an especially important part. Since changes in the rates may be large, successful speculation can yield a high rate of profit. Under the influence of speculative dealing, the rate of exchange may be steadied at a level which in the view of the speculators will equate the prospective non-speculative supply and demand. If, however, there is complete uncertainty as to the future, speculation may induce violent fluctuations. If the currency is moving in a certain direction, e.g. downwards, speculators will anticipate the future, and the present rate will tend to stand, not at a point that balances present non-speculative supply and demand, but at one which is expected to balance non-speculative supply and demand three months, six months or a year hence. This process was amply illustrated in the external "undervaluation" of the inflating currencies after the first war. Relatively to existing non-speculative supply and demand, their prices in terms of stable currencies were permanently too low; but in relation to what was destined to happen in the ensuing year, the present undervaluation was often moderate.

When a currency can move freely in the foreign exchange market, the two stabilizing forces referred to in § 3 largely cease to operate. Thus a certain drop in the quotation does not necessarily provoke purchases, there being no fixed floor, but may equally well stimulate sales. The drop may make most people think that there is likely to be a still further fall. Changes in the Bank Rate and market rates of interest become totally inoperative, since the differences between interest rates in different financial centres are usually negligible in comparison with the risk of loss through a downward movement of the exchange rate in the course of ninety days. People will buy a freely floating currency to cover foreseen commitments or for speculative reasons; but they will not do so with the idea of gaining $\frac{1}{4}\%$ or even $\frac{1}{2}\%$ on the interest rate for 90 days. Sales will be similarly governed.

Sterling became inconvertible under the stress of circumstances in September, 1931. The inability of the Bank Rate to influence its quotation in the period 1931–39 was, although unfortunate in itself, paradoxically a reason for not restoring convertibility, as could easily have been done. For the authorities were very anxious to maintain an extremely low Bank Rate in order to alleviate domestic unemployment, which was very large, and feared that a restoration of convertibility might put them into a position in which they would be obliged to raise the Bank Rate in certain circumstances.

§ 6. **Exchange Equalization Funds.** In order to obviate excessive fluctuations, when there is no par of exchange, the monetary authorities may institute machinery for steadying the exchange market. The British Equalization Account, established under the Treasury in April 1932, was the most important and successful example of this. Its object was to reduce short-term fluctuations due to the following two causes:

(a) A country whose foreign balance of payments is equal when computed over a sufficiently long period may have discrepancies from day to day, from month to month and seasonally. This is only to be expected. The day to day totals being aggregates of a large number of individual transactions carried out from motives of private advantage, it is not to be expected that discrepancies will not occur. In the ordinary operation of the gold standard these are made good in part by the movements of funds induced by small fluctuations in the rates of exchange, in part by movements of funds in response to changes in the relative levels of short-term interest rates and finally by movements of gold. In the absence of a gold par small movements in the exchange rates lose their significance and funds will not flow to take advantage of small differences in the rates of interest, since attempts to do this involve exposure to exchange risks of greater magnitude.

(b) After 1931 there was a growing tendency for short-term funds to move from country to country in search for security and in response to political alarms and rumours. Lack of confidence in the government led citizens to seek a temporary haven for their money abroad; a restoration of confidence led to repatriation. Such movements amounted to hundreds of millions of pounds sterling, and these, being sometimes concentrated within a comparatively short period, dwarfed the flow of money arising out of normal trading or investment activities. It was the purpose of the Exchange Account to prevent such movements creating a violent disturbance in the rates of foreign exchange. If foreign money flowed in or domestic money was repatriated, the Account bought sufficient gold or foreign exchange to offset the movement and obviate exchange fluctuation, which it would otherwise have entailed. This purchase also served to create a reserve out of which gold or foreign exchange could be sold in the event of a reverse movement. Whether the stabilizing flows induced by the gold standard mechanism would have sufficed to offset large movements of funds of this type, which came to be known as "hot money", is doubtful.

It is to be noted, however, that, in pursuit of its objectives, the Exchange Equalization Account had to build up a gold reserve which would suffice, not only to cover any likely outflow of hot money, but also to cover those seasonal and occasional excesses of demand over supply of foreign currencies that, under the gold standard, had been covered by private operators actuated by exchange fluctuations within the gold points and by Bank Rate variations. And so a paradox arose: although Britain abandoned the gold standard for the time being in 1931, a far larger gold reserve had to be maintained in the following years than had ever been known before; gold was now needed to do the work formerly done by private short-term funds in making up the balance of payments from time to time.

This paradox remains under the somewhat different systems operated by most countries since the second war. Although most countries now have pars of exchange, there have been obstacles to the re-introduction of the free movement of short-term funds, and there has not been the absolute confidence in the durability of the pars, which, as indicated above, would be needful to bring back into operation the system of stabilization through private action. Consequently much larger gold reserves have been considered desirable than formerly. This has occurred at a time when the value of the monetary gold in the world has greatly fallen by comparison with the value of trade flowing, so that reserves have been very short in relation to need, and this in turn has been responsible for the unduly frequent occurrence of "crises". This points to the need for a revaluation of gold in terms of currencies; it also points to the need for the reintroduction, if possible, and conformably with other objectives of policy, of the stabilizing mechanisms of the gold standard. Another paradox has arisen. A fixed par of exchange has a number of disadvantages, which will presently be discussed; its supreme advantage is that it should automatically induce an equalizing flow of short-term funds and thus make it possible for a country to run smoothly on a fairly narrow gold reserve. The various countries maintaining fixed pars have had the disadvantages, without so far having been able to avail themselves to a great extent of the supreme advantage. It is hoped, however, that this situation is now (1956) improving.

In addition to the discrepancies arising under the foregoing heads, (a) and (b), it is possible for there to be a persistent tendency towards a passive balance of total payments, either because there is a passive balance on current account not fully offset by foreign loans to the country or because, while there is an active balance on current account, residents in the country choose to make net foreign investments of greater value. There may be a persistent tendency to an active balance in converse circumstances.

The fundamental forces governing the state of the total balance are discussed in the following chapters. The Exchange Account did not seek to check downward or upward movements in the foreign exchange rate thought likely to redress a fundamental disequilibrium. This policy of allowing flexibility in the exchange rates in the long-run is consistent with resolute attempts to even out temporary fluctuations. Thus it may be possible to get the best of both worlds.

By 1936 it had become fairly evident that it was desirable for France, despite her painful experiences of inflation and devaluation in the 'twenties, to allow the franc to depreciate or to devalue it in terms of gold, the United States, Britain and the whole sterling area, and a number of other countries having already done so. To give face to the French government in taking this unpopular measure, the United States and Britain entered into a Tripartite Monetary Agreement with her, for mutual action to support each other's currencies. In practice this commitment meant that the British were bound to keep sterling steady—the U.S. and France both having fixed, though devalued, pars—or at least not let it rise over much against the franc and the dollar; thus it seemed that she had very nearly returned to the gold standard—though without the advantages mentioned above—until the very near menace of war in Europe (and renewed franc troubles) made the authorities feel that they must allow sterling to move downwards.

§ 7. **Balance of Payments Further Considered.** The balance of payments arising on both sides of the account under (i) and (iv) (*a*), as specified in § 1 above, is called the balance of payments "on account of goods and services".[1] If this account considered by itself is positive a country is sometimes said to have a favourable balance, and, if negative, an unfavourable one.

These words have an "emotive" tendency, suggesting in the former case that the country is doing well and in the latter doing badly. An emotive implication governed by the balance on current account would not necessarily be right, and in

---

[1] This is sometimes called the balance on current account. More often this phrase is used to include all recurrent items other than capital.

common speech the words "favourable" and "unfavourable", when used of balances of payments, do not always refer to the current account. The use of words of emotive import does not necessarily imply what is called a "value judgment", although it may; rather what common language is seeking to suggest, especially in its use of "unfavourable", is that there is a situation that will have to be corrected.

Consider item (iii). If the "gifts" consist of a steady stream of remittances by emigrants to their home country, which is expected to continue, there is no reason why these should not be included in striking a balance prior to assessing whether the position of the country is "favourable" or "unfavourable". If the country is in "unfavourable" balance, before including these remittances, but in equal balance after including them, there is no reason to regard its position as "unfavourable"; in such a condition no correction is called for. But if the gifts consist of such payments as "Marshall Aid", generously devised to help countries in their post-war difficulties, then they should be excluded in striking the balance; a country whose balance is only rendered equal by the inclusion of such a receipt should be deemed to be in unfavourable balance, because a correction will be required in due course.

In this wider sense the favourable or unfavourable balance is to be assessed after the inclusion not only of payments on account of goods and services, but of all payments that may be deemed to be normal or continuing. The difficulty of determining normalcy in this connexion centres on item (ii)—capital movements. It may be quite normal for an under-developed country to be in receipt of payments arising out of investment by foreigners in its borders year by year; it is true that in the long run a correction will be required, namely when the country ceases to be relatively under-developed. But that is a longer run than is relevant to the usage of the words we are considering. A classic instance is the United States, which in the early part of the nineteenth century attracted foreign capital for its development; during that period the inflow of payments on capital account should have been included *before* assessing whether its aggregate balance was favourable or unfavourable, although after the passage of a number of decades its situation in this regard was destined to be reversed.

What we seek to include before striking the balance are those payments, whether on current or capital account, which may be regarded as motived by natural and continuing commercial and financial considerations. These need not be solely payments on account of private enterprise. In the modern situation governments or official agencies may deem it part of a continuing policy to promote and be responsible for a flow of capital to under-developed countries.

What is quite certain is that the movement of short-term funds, to the extent that this is due to exchange fluctuations between official points or to interest rate differentials designed to have a short-term influence on the balance, should *not* be included. Such payments are the result of an unequal balance and only occur because there is an unequal balance; they act as a substitute for the flow of gold; such movements are much to be desired in an era like the present when the supply of monetary gold is gravely inadequate. These movements must be regarded as balancing items and should be excluded in striking the balance.

It is probably inevitable that the words "favourable balance" will continue to be used in two senses, viz. for the balance on account of goods and services, and for the balance when certain other items, including capital items, have also been reckoned in. It will continue to be necessary to infer the sense from the context. Consider the sentence, "it is salutary that the U.S., having a favourable balance of payments, like Britain before 1914, should invest money in under-developed countries". Here favourable balance refers to balance on current account, since the sentence leaves it uncertain whether the U.S. still has a favourable balance after reckoning her foreign investment in; Britain before 1914 did not. On the other hand "the favourable balance of the U.S. is an embarrassment to other countries" clearly refers to her balance in the wider sense; otherwise her favourable balance could not be represented as an embarrassment. In neither sense must the balancing short-term capital items be reckoned in.

Unhappily for the compilation of statistics these are elusive. The International Monetary Fund has made an invaluable compilation of the balances of payments of the various countries. In the course of its work it made a heroic attempt to segregate all items, the totals of which should be deemed to indicate whether the balance in the wider sense defined above was favourable or unfavourable, the other items being labelled "compensatory official financing"; this latter included gold movements. This classification gave rise to argument about whether certain official loans were intended to be "compensatory", i.e. merely to help a country in its balance of payments troubles, or were designed as a normal contribution to the internal development of the country in question; they might have a little of both elements; and individual members of such a body as the International Bank sponsoring a loan might have different private thoughts about its true purpose. The I.M.F. has accordingly weakened in its praiseworthy attempt to make this important classification.

The word "official" was unfortunate, since in gold standard conditions, to which we are tending to return, most compensatory financing was private. More important, it is not clear whether these private compensatory movements are visibly reflected in the reported liabilities and assets of banks (or other bodies). Statisticians are familiar with what are known as "leads" and "lags" in the balance of payments, that is when payments for goods are anterior or posterior to their passage through the ports. If these leads and lags were constant through time and depended exclusively on fixed commercial habits, it would be relatively easy to relate the balance of payments to the balance of visible trade, by applying constant leads or lags to the values of recorded imports and of exports. But it is of the essence of the stabilizing or compensatory forces, such as changes of interest rates, tending to make the balance of payments more equal, to cause *changes* in the leads and lags. A notable example is provided by the German balance of 1956. But this also gives rise to a further statistical problem. A rise in a country's interest rates (relative to those abroad) makes the leads and lags in the country's foreign payments more favourable to her external balance; but the German rise of interest rates in this instance was directed exclusively to the country's internal condition and had a perverse or anti-compensatory action on its external balance. Accordingly it would seem needful in deciding whether a favourable movement in leads and lags due to an interest change was compensatory or not, to look to the motives of those whose advocacy, leading to action, caused it to come about. This looks uncommonly like hair-splitting. But in fact it is not; it is indispensable for forming a correct judgment as to whether a country's balance is unfavourable, in the sense of needing correction. The moral is that the condition of the balance cannot be read straight off the recorded statistics; these have to be interpreted in the light of collateral knowledge of the circumstances.

§ 8. **Negotiability of Currencies.** Owing to the second war there were great upheavals in monetary arrangements. Trade and the movement of capital became subject to strict control. It is not proposed to give an account of foreign exchange in wartime; but certain features of the wartime system survived for many years afterwards, and still (1956) survive in a modified form. Of these it is necessary to write.

Two main types of foreign exchange system have so far been described. Under the first foreigners acquiring the currency of a certain country are assured of being able to obtain, directly or indirectly, a fixed quantity of gold, and thereby a fixed quantity of the currency of any country on the gold standard. Currencies, and only currencies, where this condition was fulfilled were called "convertible".[1] The term

[1] The fact that not all foreigners, but only foreign Treasuries or Central Banks, were after 1933 able to obtain gold for dollars did not, except in the view of certain fanatics, require us to regard the dollar as inconvertible.

"convertible" is somewhat wider than "gold standard", since it includes the silver standard and indeed any other system whereby the authorities maintain the value of a currency by being willing to give in exchange for it a given quantity of a commodity (or of several commodities) or a given quantity of some other convertible currency.

Under the other system, formerly always called the system of "inconvertible" currency, foreigners did not have this advantage, but were free to take what they could get for the currency in a foreign exchange market, which might or might not be influenced by the operations of an Exchange Equalization Fund in the country in question.

Recently quite a different system has been developed. Under it the foreigner who acquires the currency in question is neither able to exchange it for gold or another gold-convertible currency at par, nor to sell it for what he can get for it in the market, but is restricted as to the use to which he can put it. This type of arrangement did not begin during the second world war, but some time before it during the world slump. Germany was its pioneer. For instance the foreigner might be allowed to use the currency only in discharge of a liability to residents of the country itself. Sometimes, as in the German case, restrictions on the use of the currency varied, depending upon how the foreigners came to acquire it; or depending on this also, it might be disposable at varying rates of discount; such arrangements are called multiple currency systems and these still persist in various countries, notably in Latin America.

During the war Britain, seeking to live as much on credit as possible and not to engage her manpower at home on making exports merely to pay her way—save for exports urgently required to sustain the economies of countries which were furnishing her or her allies with supplies—entered into agreements, known as Payments Agreements, with most countries, whereby sterling, accruing to them by the sale to her of goods or by the provision to her of services for her forces overseas or in any other way, was to be held by them in Special Accounts

8

and was only usable for the discharge of liabilities to the sterling area. Restrictions of this kind are properly called restrictions on negotiability.

Since the war a new usage has crept into our language whereby inconvertibility has been used to mean some limitation on negotiability. The student of economics should be warned that if he reads the word "inconvertible" in relation to currency, in any book, report, journal or newspaper written before 1945, this means simply that the authority issuing the currency was not prepared to give gold (or other gold currencies, etc.) for it at par, and does not imply any lack of right to transfer the currency to someone else. Thus between 1931 and 1939 sterling was said to be "inconvertible", although anyone holding it was perfectly entitled by British or any other law to negotiate it by transferring it to anyone else in the world for the price (in terms of other currencies) that he could get for it in the market. Since the war there was for a period some discussion of making sterling "convertible at a freely floating rate"; by pre-war usage this would be a contradiction in terms. It is not clear yet whether the new usage will persist; it is confusing, and likely to be particularly confusing to future historians.[1]

In the definitions of convertibility and negotiability given above, reference was made to foreign holders. The rights of foreigners may be deemed to give the crucial test in this matter. Some Continental writers have recently drawn a distinction between "resident convertibility" and "non-resident convertibility", usually adding that resident convertibility is necessarily comprised in convertibility proper or "full" convertibility. The British prefer to take convertibility to mean what the Continental experts call "non-resident convertibility", both because the concept of resident convertibility is unclear, and also to prevent any confusion between "convertibility"

[1] It is surprising how such a startling change of usage should have come in so quickly. In the post-war period the question of convertibility was one of sharp controversy in certain circles, and the change of usage may have been due to a desire, more probably unconscious than deliberate, to confuse the issue.

and "freedom from Exchange Control", which are two quite distinct ideas.

During the war it became illegal for residents of Britain to enter into various transactions with the outer world, notably to import certain goods, or more than specified quantities of certain goods, to spend money, or more than a specified amount of money, on foreign travel, and to invest their capital outside the sterling area. When an action is declared illegal it is always desirable to have some method of enforcing or "policing" the law. One method, although not the only method, of enforcing the prohibitions on foreign transactions of the type listed above is to make it impossible for individuals to get the money required to carry out the transactions in question. "Exchange Control" is the generic expression for laws or regulations making it impossible for individuals to get foreign currency with a view to carrying out transactions that are unlawful in themselves. If the prohibited transactions are at all extensive, it is in practice likely also to be necessary to keep a check upon what foreign currencies individuals are acquiring for perfectly lawful transactions, and, equally important, to ensure the surrender of foreign currencies acquired by the sale of exports or in other ways; if there is no such check, the path of the law breaker is all too easy.

The scope of unlawful transactions in Britain has been greatly reduced since the war, and many hope that it will be further reduced as quickly as possible. But there is one type of transaction about which there is still considerable doubt—namely whether residents can be allowed, without detriment to the economy, to invest as much of their capital abroad, especially in the United States, as suits their fancy. If it proves undesirable to remove this restriction completely, then some degree of "policing" or "Exchange Control" is likely to continue to be necessary.

How is this Exchange Control related to the idea of convertibility? We may say right away that the relation is a very distant one. Throughout the war and in the years after it, sterling was fully convertible for residents, in the sense that the resident could always convert his sterling with the British authorities, i.e. get foreign currency in exchange for his sterling from them at the official rate (at par), with a view to entering into any legal transaction with a foreigner. What he could not do was to convert his sterling with a view to illegal transactions.

The position of the foreigner (subject to exceptions as explained below) was totally different. The British authorities would not convert his sterling into gold or foreign currencies at all for any purpose whatever. Nor would they allow him to transfer his sterling to anyone outside the sterling area or his own country. (This, however, was soon made subject to a wide latitude presently to be explained.)

What of the future? The proposal to make sterling convertible means that non-resident holders will be able to obtain, directly or indirectly, gold or any foreign currencies they need in exchange for their sterling at the official rates. By the new usage but not by the old, sterling would be made "convertible" if these non-residents merely became free legally to transfer their sterling to any other country whatsoever, but had to accept any discount on it, however wide, that might obtain in the open market. This latter should more properly be called full negotiability.

For the resident, convertibility will bring no change in principle, because for the resident sterling has always been fully convertible, for all transactions not forbidden by law. Whether it will be possible to reduce the scope of prohibited transactions, e.g. the investment by British residents of their capital outside the sterling area, and whether, if so, it will be possible to get rid altogether of that form of policing the law known as "Exchange Control", are totally different questions from that of restoring convertibility.

That there is a distant cousinship, however, between Exchange Control and inconvertibility must be recognized. A State can make laws for its own citizens about what international transactions are permitted to them, and police these laws by exchange control. It cannot interfere in the same way

with the private lives of foreigners; but by restricting negotiability it imposes a kind of blanket control, making it impossible
(or difficult or unprofitable) for them to use the currency they
have acquired for any transactions whatever with third party
countries.

What are the economic effects of these arrangements? The
effect of Exchange Control on residents does not concern us
here; it is identical with the effect of the laws or regulations
(e.g., restrictions on imports or capital movements) that the
Control is designed to police.

Multiple currency arrangements tend to favour those
debit-creating transactions for which foreign currencies are
officially obtainable at lower rates of exchange and to favour
those credit-creating transactions for which the home currency
is obtainable at lower rates of exchange; and conversely. Thus
they are means of enforcing the views of the authorities in
regard to what types of international transaction they wish
citizens to enter upon. They are especially favoured by
countries where the administrative machinery is relatively
rudimentary, so that it might be difficult for them to enforce
particular regulations, such as import quotas, by overall
Exchange Control or other methods.

The effect of limiting the negotiability of the currency held
by foreigners merits special consideration. We may take the
strong case where a currency held by foreigners can only be
transferred to the home country or to other residents of the
country of its holders. This tends to force trade towards a
bi-lateral balance between the two countries. Price ratios
tend to equality as between them, but may remain different
from ratios in the outside world. Therefore it sets up a
situation in which the two countries taken together are not
engaging in all the trade with the third-party world that would
be capable of yielding gain.

How comes such a situation to arise? The country (A)
restricting transferability usually has difficulties with its overall
balance; otherwise it would not resort to this course; if it can
persuade a partner (B) in trade to accept its currency without

the right of general negotiability, it can (temporarily) run a deficit with that country without having to have a counter-vailing surplus in some other part of its trade. Then why does its partner country (B) consent to receive currency which is not negotiable outside? There are two reasons. A country seldom likes to sacrifice a profitable export trade; normally the authorities of (B) give its own traders domestic currency in exchange for the non-negotiable currency of (A), which the traders surrender; if the authorities of (B) did not do this their traders would be inclined to refuse to take payment in the non-negotiable currency of (A). It is feared that the authorities of (A) would then, rather than pay out gold on account of liabilities to (B), restrict its imports from (B). Thus (B) would run the risk of losing part of its export market in (A). Secondly (B) may be sweetened by the hope that one day its balances of the (A) country currency will become negotiable.

One well-known instance of this development was when Germany, in the rôle of country (A) above offered non-negotiable marks to Balkan countries before the war in exchange for their agricultural produce; the latter were reluctant to sacrifice this market, by refusing the German offers, and thereby perhaps to cause a local collapse of agricultural prices and reduce their citizens to distress. The great classic instance was Britain during the war; if the countries supplying Britain refused payment in non-negotiable sterling for their exports to her, where else would they find alternative markets for them? And in this case the sweetening hope was decidedly present that, after victory, the negotiability of sterling would be restored.

Restriction of negotiability gave rise to the distinction be-tween "hard" and "soft" currencies, not known in earlier days. When currencies were inconvertible (pre-war sense), but fully negotiable, they showed their relative weakness by being more depreciated in the foreign exchange market. If a country has a good overall balance, it has no motive to limit negotiability and its currency remains "hard". If a country restricts negotiability, that is usually a sign that it is tending to overall deficit; its currency will be "soft", both because it is non-negotiable and because its supply is running ahead of demand. During the war and afterwards the degree of the hardness and softness of various currencies changed from time to time, the U.S. dollar, however, remaining hard throughout. Furthermore a currency might be hard in relation to one country, while soft in relation to another.

As time proceeded, the U.S. dollar became *the* hard currency, *par excellence*; it remained continuously hard *vis-à-vis* the great majority of other currencies. In these circumstances a major purpose of non-negotiability came to be to secure that the "(B)" country (see above) did not use the "(A)" country's currency to pay its dollar debts. This solution to the dollar problem, which was developed *ad hoc* as a matter of expediency, was by no means an ideal one; for it tended to compel each country to balance its dollar account bi-laterally as best it might. In a world of well balanced multilateral trade, it is probable that some countries would normally be in deficit on dollar account, others in surplus. In conditions of general dollar shortage, the former would have an abnormally large deficit, but the latter would have some deficit also, albeit a much smaller one. The system we have outlined compelled the large deficit countries to restrict dollar imports severely while the latter might balance their dollar accounts by a small restriction only. That is not in line with the economic criterion, which requires a more or less equi-proportional restriction all round, having regard, however, to how vital to a particular country's economy are the goods which only the scarce currency country can supply.

These rather tortured currency arrangements have been connected with "discrimination" in import restrictions. When currencies were always fully negotiable, although sometimes inconvertible, a country had no motive for discrimination in import restriction on account of balance of payments difficulties. Each country was concerned with its overall balance of payments and, if in difficulties, might impose import restrictions; but since the currency of any foreign country was freely interchangeable with that of any other foreign country, nothing was to be gained by restricting imports from one rather than another country. In those days discrimination against the imports of another country could only have a political motive. (Discrimination in favour of another country might, however, be granted in return for a reciprocal advantage.) The distinction between political discrimination and that due to the genuine scarcity of a particular currency has not perhaps been sufficiently allowed for in all quarters.

The basic cause alike of the non-negotiability of currencies and of import discriminations has been the large size of the maladjustment in the balance of trade, which has been the aftermath of the second war. The authorities have had the belief, which has probably often, although not necessarily in all cases, been correct, that Bank Rate manipulations and adjustments of foreign exchange rates would not by themselves suffice to rectify an imbalance of international payments where that had become very great.

§ 9. Sterling. For a long period of history sterling has been used to finance not only the greater part of Britain's external trade, but also much trade and other payments between countries outside Britain. This was due to the world-wide ramification of Britain's investment and finance, and also to sterling having been for many generations the best regulated currency in the world. These two facts were doubtless interconnected. Before the war all the currencies of the Commonwealth, apart from Canada, were so closely linked with sterling, that, although they might have different names, e.g. the Indian rupee, they should properly be regarded as sterling currencies.

When Britain departed from the gold standard in 1931, a number of other countries outside the Commonwealth, notably the Scandinavian, voluntarily did likewise, preferring to hold their various currencies at a fixed par with sterling, rather than

with gold.[1] The sterling Commonwealth along with these
countries became known as the "sterling area", membership
of which, however, varied a little from time to time.

On the outbreak of war Britain decided that it would be
necessary to limit by law the right of British citizens to take
their capital out of the sterling area. Law unfortunately
requires definition. Thus the sterling area had reluctantly
to be defined. It was constituted by the Commonwealth
apart from Canada and one or two other countries (e.g.
Iceland, and, for a considerable period, Egypt).

For the sterling area, sterling has since 1939 been convertible
in the same broad sense that it has been convertible for British
residents throughout.   Sterling area members could get sterling
accounts in London converted into foreign currencies
(including dollars) at the official rates. But residents of the
whole sterling area have been subject to restrictions on external
transactions allowed (although not identical restrictions to
those imposed on British residents), and subject also to
Exchange Control, as required to police their own restrictions.
Furthermore there has been co-operation between members of
the sterling area as to the severity of the restrictions to be
imposed from time to time, having regard to the balance of
payments of the area as a whole. This has been secured by
meetings between the Finance Ministers.

Sterling held by the countries known as American Account
countries—the United States, Canada, Venezuela, Cuba and
some other Latin-American countries—has throughout been
fully convertible and negotiable. The reason for this favourable treatment was that the countries in question were strong
enough to obtain it. It will be remembered that in the account
above (§ 8) of the relation between the "A" and "B" countries,
the B country had some element of weakness—it did not wish
to lose exports and was willing to live on hope. The American

[1] An earlier instance of this was when Hungary, having restored the
pengo in 1924 after the first war, decided to give it a fixed par with sterling,
which had not yet been restored to the gold standard, rather than with
gold.

Account countries, on the contrary, if not given the privileges of convertibility and negotiability, would simply have insisted on payment in dollars.

During the war bilateral agreements were made between Britain and most other countries and their sterling holdings could only be used for payment to the sterling area. But shortly afterwards, a number of countries were grouped together in what was known as the transferable account system. Their sterling holdings might be used for payment to the sterling area, or to other members of the transferable account group.

One further category of post-war sterling must be mentioned. At the end of the war the sterling balances held outside Britain amounted to a very high figure. Some of these were blocked (officially "restricted"). This was altogether different from the treatment of the majority of sterling balances which were usable for payment to the sterling area; the blocked balances could not be used at all for any purpose. They were almost exclusively inside the sterling area and never amounted to more than a lesser part of the total. These balances were politely labelled "No. 2 accounts". Much the most important were those of India and Egypt. They have since been greatly reduced, part of the former going as a contribution to the Colombo Plan.

From the outset free markets arose in which sterling of limited negotiability was exchanged for gold or other currencies. From the British point of view these dealings were irregular. The sellers were those for whom their sterling was redundant; the buyers were glad to acquire it at a discount against the official rate. Quotations for various different kinds of sterling were established. After the transferable account system was inaugurated, transferable account sterling became the most important. But the sterling held by each country with which Britain had a bi-lateral agreement (Saudi-Arabian sterling, etc.) was quoted, as well as other varieties such as sterling held by foreigners who had sold sterling securities and were only allowed to use it for the purchase of other sterling securities.

It cannot be said that these various quotations in any sense reflected the true equilibrium value of sterling. Those who used the market did so to avoid or evade the intentions of the British regulations and were a limited class. But the variations in the market rates might give some indication of the trend of opinion about British prospects.

For periods after the war these sterlings were at heavy discounts, which were a temptation to buyers to use the free markets. An American, for instance, desiring to buy a commodity from the sterling area might arrange to have it invoiced to another country, say Saudi Arabia, so that the Exchange Control would think all was in order when the sterling area exporter received payment from that country. But the commodity would not go to that country at all. The Saudi-Arabian would have disposed of unwanted sterling at a discount; the American would have acquired sterling below the official rate; the Bank of England would be deprived of the dollars that would otherwise have accrued to it by the sale of a sterling area commodity to an American through proper channels, and would only have the inferior satisfaction of having a sterling liability to Saudi-Arabia reduced. It was incumbent on the British authorities to check such practices. But when one method was stopped a more devious one was found; and many alternative methods were devised by those versed in these matters. These methods became very rife in bad periods for sterling, like the spring of 1949.

The discount at which the sterling was sold did not, however, represent pure gain for the buyer of it, since the necessary intermediaries had to be paid for their pains. As the years wore on two forces tended to reduce the discount on sterling sold in the free markets, the reduction in the surplus of available sterling over requirements for it held outside the sterling area, and the prospect of convertibility—it was foolish to part with sterling at a substantial discount if with a little patience one would later be able to cash it at par.

In the winter of 1953–54 free market quotations for transferable sterling were at times up to the (lower) official rate for sterling.   In the spring of 1954 the British authorities brought all countries outside the American Account area—with one or two minor exceptions—within the transferable account system. Later in the year the prospect for convertibility declined somewhat, partly owing to fears connected with the temporary American recession then proceeding, and a more substantial discount on transferable sterling developed again, and with it undesirable commodity operations.

On February 24, 1955, the British authorities decided to intervene in the free markets to support transferable sterling and to hold the rate for it so near to the rate for official sterling, as not to leave a profitable margin for commodity operations. Since that date it may be said that transferable account sterling, which comprises the great mass of all sterling outside the dollar and sterling areas, has been *de facto* convertible (and negotiable), subject to a discount against official sterling of only 2 or 3 U.S. cents to the pound.

Discussion of the International Monetary Fund is deferred to Chapter VIII.

CHAPTER VI

THE BALANCE OF TRADE

§ 1. The Classical Doctrine. The foregoing chapter was concerned with the mechanism by which international payments are cancelled against one another and by which seasonal or random discrepancies in the balance are made good. It is necessary to consider the deeper question of the forces which tend to keep the balance even in the longer run.

A retrospect of "classical" doctrine is given at this point, because, it must be confessed, the classical writers presented a neater solution of the problem than any which can be given with confidence to-day. The modern view comprises a clearer and more thorough understanding of some of the factors involved but does not lead up to so compact a theory. The classical writers were by no means agreed on all particulars; while Ricardo had a more satisfactory theory, J. S. Mills's gift for exposition ensured a wider currency for his own views, which have since been regarded as constituting the classical theory *par excellence*.

First suppose a gold standard in operation. If the sum of all payments in is not exactly equal to that of payments out on current and capital accounts, the difference is balanced by an international flow of gold. The consequence of gold inflow will be a tendency of prices to rise in the receiving country and to fall outside; conversely with an outflow. The consequence of this in turn is a reduction in the range of goods which the country can offer at the prices ruling elsewhere, which entails a shrinkage of her exports and an expansion of her imports. So long as the gold flows in, this process continues, the sum of payments in declines and the sum of payments out increases. This tends to reduce the active balance of payments and finally

111

to extinguish it. At this point gold flows no longer, and equilibrium is reached.

Certain difficulties may next be considered in turn.

(i) The theory assumes that an inflow of gold tends to raise prices (and an outflow to reduce them). This is connected with the Quantity Theory of money. The quantity of money in the country is supposed to be connected with the quantity of gold in the country. An inflow of gold will, unless the banks deliberately take counteracting measures, increase the quantity of money, and an outflow will decrease it. The quantity of money in the country may, however, be large by comparison with the quantity of gold. In the event of an outflow, the reserve of gold may be exhausted before the equilibrium is reached. To meet such a situation the banking system may have to supplement the effect of the outflow and make an extra reduction in the quantity of money by curtailing loans. It is quite in conformity with the general idea of the classical doctrine, to suppose that supplementary banking action of this kind may be necessary.

Indeed according to one view the banking system will tend to keep a fixed ratio between the total quantity of bank money and the quantity of gold in the system. In this case the supplementary action would be taken automatically as a result of what might be called the standing orders for working the gold standard.

(ii) On many occasions since the first world war countries on the gold standard have not worked it in this manner. On the contrary, they have taken action to neutralize the movements of gold; this has either been through "open-market operations" of the central bank, which sells an equivalent amount of securities when gold comes in and so prevents the inflow from increasing the quantity of money in the country and buys when gold goes out, or, as in the case of the U.S.A. on one occasion, by government measures to sterilize the gold.

Under such a system the classical doctrine would not lead one to expect international payments to tend to a balance;

and its exponents have pointed with some satisfaction to these measures as giving a perfectly good reason why an even balance should in fact have failed from time to time to materialize.

It is possible to suspect, however, that this explanation of the failure to balance explains too much, that trade has in fact balanced *better* than it ought to have, if the operation of gold flows on relative national price levels were indeed the sole means of securing a balance.

(iii) How is the Quantity Theory related to the price levels of the three categories of goods, defined in Chapter IV? So far as A goods are concerned there are no separate national price levels (apart from the effects of tariffs, etc.), so that in that field the theory breaks down or at least requires restating. The prices of B goods may vary from country to country; it is important to emphasize that the competitive power of the home country will only be reduced (or increased) if money costs of production are raised (or lowered); if the alleged force of the gold flow is to be effective in this sphere, it must operate on money costs of production. C goods do not enter into the balance of trade, but their prices may operate through their effect on the cost of production of other goods. How may these forces be reduced to the simplest terms?

Consideration of A goods may give the clue. Here a price differential is ruled out. None the less, the flow of gold may influence the balance of trade in them in two ways. (a) If there is an increase of *activity* in the receiving country in consequence of the inflow, and a higher aggregate income for this reason, more A goods may be bought and imports therefore increased. (b) If factors come to receive higher rates of money rewards in consequence of the inflow, they may be able to afford more A goods, the price level of which is presumed to be unchanged, both because they have a higher money income per head and possibly because other available goods will have become more expensive owing to higher money costs. This would make for higher imports. On the other hand, with the rise of factor rewards, costs of production will be higher, and the marginal producers may be squeezed out of business; this makes for lower exports. These two considerations, increase of activity and higher rates of money rewards, summarize the possible effects of a gold inflow on the balance of trade in A goods. The same is true of B goods; the possible change of their price level in the process may be regarded merely as an incidental by-product of it.

Thus the classical theory has been restated, having regard to the three categories of goods, and the required operation of the gold flow is seen to depend on its success in affecting (a) the level of activity in the country and (b) the level of monetary rewards. It was not characteristic of classical thought to pay much attention to the level of activity. This matter is considered in paragraph (v) below. In interpreting their doctrine primary emphasis should be placed on the level of monetary rewards.

Now in the modern world this level is notoriously somewhat sticky, and it may be hazarded that in the nineteenth century it was more sticky than the pure classical doctrine of the balance of trade implied. Exponents of the doctrine here again tend to express satisfaction since the stickiness of rewards may serve to explain why the theory of the balance has not been precisely fulfilled. And here again it is legitimate to suspect that the explanation over-explains. Trade has probably balanced more than it ought to have done, if the ready adjustment of rates of monetary reward to factors were the sole force at work securing such a balance.

(iv) Classical theory tended to assume that the international flow of investment intended to be permanent was governed by rival prospects of profit and security in different countries, and that it should consequently be regarded as an independent factor in the situation to which other items in the balance of payments would have to adjust themselves. Thus if the capitalists of a country in search of higher profits chose to invest £100 million per annum abroad, gold would flow in such a way and have such an effect on relative price structures, that the investing country would automatically find itself with a favourable balance of trade of the value of £100 million.[1]

Recently some doubt has been cast on the correctness of this. The flow of capital may not be so independent. It is possible that the capitalists of a country may be tempted to invest (or borrow) abroad precisely because of the conditions which the active (or passive) balance of trade has brought about. This view will be elaborated in a later section (§ 5).

(v) It is necessary to return to the problem set in the beginning of Chapter III—what are the conditions in which the productive services of a country will be fully employed? Classical thought tended to assume full employment in some sense. But suppose that this condition fails?

The gold flow was explicitly relied on to secure a level of monetary rewards to factors, such as to make trade balance, it being implicitly assumed that factors were fully employed. But it is clear that the level of factor rewards required to secure a balance of trade will be different according to whether or not the factors are fully employed. If a country is working with a high level of unemployment, it will concentrate on producing the goods in which it has the greatest comparative advantage; if it wishes full employment, it will have to employ the residual factors in less profitable fields. Consequently a balance of trade can be secured with unemployment, at a higher level of money rewards than would be feasible if the necessity of full employment were postulated.

Now if we rely on the gold flow to secure a balance of trade through its operation on the rate of money rewards—assuming for the sake of argument that those are readily adjustable—what particular level of employment will it secure? There is clearly a missing link in the argument. The flow of gold clearly cannot automatically secure *both* a balance of trade *and* a full

[1] Traditional theory has indeed assumed a balancing movement of short-term funds; this was dealt with in ch. V. The argument of this chapter is concerned with movements likely to rectify a permanent tendency towards an uneven balance, not with temporary movements due to be reversed at a later date.

9

level of employment. Some determining force must have been left out of account. This matter is taken up in § 6.

If the assumption of the gold standard is removed, classical doctrine expects that the rates of foreign exchange will, in due course, be adjusted to a "natural" level at which the supply and demand for foreign currencies balance. This theory is simpler. We no longer have to consider how a flow of gold suffices to alter the rates of money rewards to factors; the relation of these money rewards to the level of prices in the outer world is automatically changed by the change in the foreign exchange rates. Thus the difficulties i–iii enumerated above do not arise.

But difficulties iv and v remain. The rate of exchange at which trade balances will be different according to the level of employment assumed to exist. The relation of the rate of money rewards at home to the world price level does not give a unique rate of foreign exchange. There will be various rates according to the level of employment assumed. Which rate does the balance of supply and demand establish? Presumably the rate appropriate to the level of employment actually existing. Suppose now that the quotations of the home currency are lowered by artificial intervention and that in consequence employment at home is stimulated. The new rate will make trade balance at the new level of employment. It is, in fact, just as "natural" as the old rate. Yet it might never have been reached save through artificial intervention. In fact when variations in employment are reckoned as a possibility, there is no "unique" natural rate.

The inadequacy of the theory may be shown as follows. Suppose that an equilibrium is disturbed by the loss of a foreign market. The loss of exports, by weakening the demand for sterling will weaken the foreign exchange quotations of sterling. How far will the fall go? The theory does not tell us. If producers take a bad view of the depression likely to result from the fall of exports, production may be curtailed all round, incomes reduced and therewith the purchase of imports, so that a new balance of trade is achieved with the foreign exchange rate very near to its old level and a considerable increase of unemployment in the country. If on the other hand producers refuse to be depressed and production, the level of income and of imports are all maintained, the foreign exchange rates under the pressure of the continued excess of supply over demand will move downwards till a balance of trade is achieved at the old level of employment. The fall in the exchange will improve the relative position of home producers whether competing with foreigners in home or foreign markets and thus fill the gap caused by the loss of the particular export market. Employment may be maintained at its old level. Now the traditional theory does not and cannot tell us which of these things will happen, since what does happen on our showing depends upon the optimism or pessimism of producers. Either upshot is equally consistent with the traditional theory.

Optimism and pessimism were here dragged in as a *deus ex machina*, not as necessarily being the factors which do in the real world determine the course of events, but only to show that the classical theory is inadequate to determine which of the two alternative kinds of equilibrium is achieved. It is to be hoped that modern theory may avail to give a more precise explanation.

The failure of the classical theory is not due to any logical inadequacy, but only to the fact that its logic requires the postulate that full employment will in any event be maintained.

The relation of this argument to the general theory of comparative costs may be understood by a reference back to Chapter IV, § 5 and 6, where the relation of the price level of factors of production inside a country to the world price level is discussed, taking the possibility of unemployment into account.

§ 2. Equilibrium in Simplified Conditions. It is necessary to approach the problem by stages. In the first stage it will be supposed that all payments are in respect of goods and services traded. Since it is dangerous to consider foreign transactions in isolation and their inter-connexion with national production and consumption must always be borne in mind, it will be supposed in this stage that, not only is there no foreign investment, but no domestic investment either. Individuals and corporate bodies in their capacity of final consumers spend the whole of their incomes. There is no addition to the capital goods of the country.

In this stage it will be shown that trade may be expected to balance without the intervention of a gold flow. Indeed the simplified assumptions rule out such a flow. Now although an automatic balance of this sort will no longer appear when the simplifying assumptions are removed, yet the kind of force here considered will be in operation subject to various complications. The reader may properly regard the argument as suggesting that the later classical writers tended to make the gold flow play an unduly important part in the establishment of an even balance.

Consumers' expenditure is divided between home-made goods and imports, in which must be included the imported raw materials contained in home-made goods. The total national income is derived from the sale of goods to consumers at home and exports. (It is assumed that the reader is aware of the special problems connected with the treatment of taxation in computing national income, to avoid double counting.) Income derived from the sale of goods to consumers at home is equal to the amount of income devoted to their purchase. And since total income is equal to total expenditure, the value of exports is equal to that of imports.

But what will the value of exports be? This depends on four circumstances: (i) the money rates of reward to factors of production at home, (ii) the efficiency of factors of production at home, (iii) prices and demand in the outer world and (iv) the profit element. (i) and (ii) together determine the cost of production at home. By comparing this with the prices ruling in the outer world, the quantity and value of the goods which it is possible to export at any given level of profit are determined. What profit will producers insist on? This

may depend in part upon past history as well as future prospects. If capital has already at the point of time under
consideration been invested in a particular line of production,
the producer may be content with any positive rate of profit
that he can get. If on the other hand a fresh investment of
capital is required, attention will be paid to the current rate of
interest, the degree of risk involved and future prospects. The
smaller the degree of risk and the better the prospects, the
lower is the rate of current profit which will induce him to
make the investment. Consideration of the influence of profit
indicates that current conditions do not alone suffice to determine the value and volume of goods that will be exported.
This proviso with regard to profit having been made, it will for
the sake of simplicity be neglected in the following paragraphs.
It will be assumed that the level of exports is determined by the
other three elements in the situation only, which may be
described by the single expression, the relation of the efficiency
rewards of factors at home to the prices and demand in the
outer world. The words "and demand" are inserted to cover
the case of B goods, about which it is not always possible to
assume that there is a single ruling price. Nevertheless as,
owing to repeated use, brevity is desirable, the expression "the
world price level" will often be employed simpliciter; it must
be remembered that this is taken to include "state of demand"
for those goods (B) which are marketed in conditions of
imperfect competition and that the prices referred to are those
of the goods in which exporters are in fact in a position to
compete with foreign producers in the places where competition
is proceeding.

If the rates of efficiency reward at home and the world price
level can be regarded as given factors in the situation, and if a
gold standard is in operation, not only the level of exports but
also the total level of income at home stand determined in the
following manner.

Let Y stand for total income, let E stand for the value of
exports, as determined by the circumstances enumerated above,
and i for the proportion of income devoted to goods made

abroad (including the imported raw materials in home-made goods). Then

$$i\,Y = E$$

$$\text{or } Y = \frac{1}{i}\,(E).$$

Thus if the value of E is given, as supposed above, and the value of i is also known, the level of income may be deduced. This is indeed self-evident, but it may assist the reader to trace the matter out step by step Let him begin with the income earned by the exporting fraternity. They earn income equal to E and spend $(1-i)$E on home-made goods. The producers of these home-made goods earn income equal to $(1-i)$E and spend in their turn a fraction $(1-i)$ of what they earn $(1-i)$E on home-made goods. Thus they spend $(1-i)(1-i)$E on home-made goods. Thus in turn another set of people earn $(1-i)(1-i)$E by producing these and spend a corresponding fraction on home-made goods. Thus the *total* amount earned by those producing home-made goods is

$$(1-i)E+(1-i)^2E+(1-i)^3E+ \ldots$$

This is an infinite series, but the sum is not infinite. By the use of elementary algebra the sum is found to be

$$\frac{1}{i}\,E - E.$$

But exporters earn income equal to E. Therefore total income is equal to

$$\frac{1}{i}\,E.$$

This method of analysing total income is known as the "multiplier" method. It consists essentially in dividing income into two parts, one part of which is derived from the receipts of income spenders and the other part, the absolute amount of which is taken to be known, is derived from another source. Total income may be deduced if it is known what proportion of their receipts income receivers spend in such a way that it does not flow back to other income receivers. The reciprocal of this proportion $\left(\frac{1}{i}\text{ above}\right)$ is known as the multiplier. The part of income not derived from income spenders and taken to be known and given may be called the base. The method will be used again in the following sections with other multipliers and bases. It is undoubtedly a valuable method of approach to the problem of the balance of trade.

Next it is desirable to examine what happens in the event of a disturbance in the fundamental conditions which determine the value of E. Suppose that, other things remaining the same, there is an improvement in productive efficiency in some other country in respect of goods which, say, England, exports, e.g. in the Japanese cotton piece-goods industry, and a consequent shrinkage in a foreign market. This involves some loss of advantage which England was formerly able to derive from her foreign trade and a deterioration in her position. Two kinds of adjustment are possible: (i) the rewards to factors may be adjusted so as to keep productive resources in reasonably full employment; (ii) factors may be allowed to go out of employment.

(i) The reduction of money rewards may serve to maintain full employment in two ways. By increasing the quantity of goods which it is now profitable to export at prices realizable in foreign markets, it goes some way to offset the initial fall in E. By reducing the prices of home-made goods competing with foreign goods in home markets it may increase the proportion of income spent upon them and so the multiplier. Thus suppose initially that total income is represented by 100, exports by 10, and $\frac{1}{10}$ of income is spent on imports, the multiplier thus being 10. Suppose that the loss of the market reduces exports to 9. A reduction of rewards will serve to maintain employment if it can re-stimulate exports to $9\frac{1}{2}$ and by lowering the relative price of home-made goods raise the multiplier to $10\frac{10}{19}$. Total income will then stand as before at 100 of which $\frac{1}{10\frac{10}{19}}$ making $9\frac{1}{2}$ units will be spent on imports.

Trade will balance as before, but at a lower volume of turnover. If there is, initially, unemployment in Japan the stimulus to it, and therefore to Japanese imports, may operate directly or indirectly by triangular trade on English exports and thus lessen the amount of reduction in rewards required in England to maintain full employment.

If the country is on a gold standard or, in the absence of a gold standard, is committed to the policy of maintaining her rates of exchange with all or most other countries stable, the reduction in rewards must take the form of an outright money reduction. Otherwise it may be brought about through a depreciation in the value of her currency in terms of other currencies. The latter method of securing reduction can be carried out with greater ease and equity as between different interests; it is discussed in a subsequent chapter.[1]

(ii) If real rewards are not reduced, what will the nature of the new equilibrium be? Full equilibrium in one sense of the term will not be achieved, since there must be some unemployment in the new situation. But there will be a new equilibrium in which receipts and expenditure, and exports and imports balance. In the new position the volume and *a fortiori* the value of exports will be reduced. It is necessary to examine the repercussions in the industries producing for the home market. Let us retain the supposition that individuals spend the whole of their incomes, neither adding to nor taking from their monetary holdings. In this case the loss of incomes in the export industries will be accompanied by a loss of incomes in the industries producing for the home market sufficient to reduce the purchase of imports by the amount that income from exports has fallen off. Thus, provided that consumers do not spend more than they receive, purchasing power will be automatically reduced by a sufficient amount to entail a reduction in imports equal to that in exports.

This may be traced out. Suppose an initial loss of income in the export industries of £p. The individuals involved spend £p less. This reduction is divided among the two main classes

[1] Ch. VII.

of expenditure. If expenditure on imports is reduced by $£q_1$, that on home produced goods is reduced by $£p-q_1$. The income of the industries producing for the home market is now reduced by $£p-q_1$ and individuals in these industries will spend less; if they spend $£q_2$ less on exports, they will spend $£p-q_1-q_2$ less on home produced goods, and there will be a further consequential reduction of incomes in industries producing for the home markets of $£p-q_1-q_2$. This entails a further reduction of expenditure on both categories. Reduction of incomes in the industries producing for the home markets will proceed by the progressive transfer of reduction, until there is no more reduction to transfer. This happens when $£p-(q_1+q_2+...)$ is zero, i.e. when

$$q_1+q_2+..=p.^1$$

But the left-hand side of this equation is the sum of all the reductions in expenditure on imports, while p is the initial loss of income from exports. Thus the reduction in imports is equal to the reduction in exports. The result that, provided no one spends more than he receives in income, total income will be reduced sufficiently to curtail expenditure on imports by the amount that exports have declined has absolute generality. Moreover, the whole process is simultaneous, so that the transition from one equilibrium to the other occurs without lapse of time. Far-reaching complications arise, when the simplifying suppositions of this enquiry do not hold. A clear understanding of this most simple and fundamental type of case is a necessary preliminary to the study of complications.

Thus even if rewards in home industries are not reduced, a balance of trade will automatically be secured without the intervention of a gold flow. The contention sometimes put forward by exponents of traditional theory that if rewards to factors are not sufficiently reduced initially, a gold outflow will proceed until they are, is seen to be without foundation in these simplified conditions.

[1] The series on the left-hand side of this equation will be infinite, since q_r is always less than $p-(q_1+..+q_{r-1})$.

This conclusion may be viewed with satisfaction in view of the warning given in Chapter I, § 2. "Theories regarding the mechanism by which the national balance of payments is maintained may be tested by applying them to any arbitrarily defined area. If they implicitly assume in every such area the presence of a mechanism which does not in fact exist, they are properly suspect."

§ 3. Balance of Payments on Current Account.

The equilibrium position when there are other items on current account[1] in the foreign balance may next be considered. Such items are interest and profit on foreign investments, gifts, indemnity payments. If capital movements are still excluded, then in equilibrium a passive balance of trade is offset by an active balance on the other items and vice versa. Imports are equal to the income from exports plus the net active foreign balance on other items. The greater this net active balance the larger *ceteris paribus* will the total income of the community be. If F stands for the net active balance on other items,

$$Y = \frac{1}{i}(E+F).$$

Thus a rise of £100 p.a. in F will, *ceteris paribus*, not merely increase Y by £100 p.a. but by $\frac{£100}{i}$ p.a. The receipt of £100 will be balanced in part by the expenditure on imports of its recipients, in part by that of those consequentially given new employment in the industries producing for the home market.

If a reduction in F occurs the opposite results follow. This may be illustrated by supposing that, on a condition in which foreign payments balance, there supervenes the necessity to make an indemnity payment. The people vote the required sum by taxation. Suppose that there is no change in world prices or rewards to factors at home and consequently no

---

[1] Used in the wider sense referred to in the footnote on p. 94.

increase in exports. The people will have less money to spend by the amount of the tax they have voted. There will at once be some curtailment of the purchase of imports by the tax-payers and of imported raw materials by those producing goods for the tax-payers. This primary reduction in imports will not be sufficient to cover the indemnity, for presumably only part of the income lost by the additional taxation would have gone to the purchase of imported goods and materials. There will also be a reduction in the purchase of home-made goods. This will lead to a reduction in domestic employment and to a further curtailment of imports owing to the loss of purchasing power by those thrown out of work. The un-employment will be extended progressively until the reduction of imports through loss of purchasing power is sufficient to cover the indemnity.

The unemployment is not, however, inevitable. It can be cured by the factors of production consenting to take lower rewards for their services. If sufficient cuts are made exports may be increased by the full amount of the indemnity, and if that happens the unemployment will disappear. How drastic the cuts required are will depend largely on the elasticity of demand and supply of the country's goods; the greater the elasticity the smaller the cuts required.[1] It will also depend on the nature of the exports. If they consist largely of B goods, more drastic cuts will probably be required than if they con-sisted largely of A goods. For the indemnity payment shifts the demand for goods in general from the tax-payers of the paying country to the tax-payers of the receiving country. This shift in demand will tend to give the producers of competing B goods in the indemnity receiving country a marketing advan-tage over those in the indemnity paying country. Thus the paying country will have to cut the price of its B goods relatively to that of the receiving country's B goods by a sufficient amount, which may be large, to tempt buyers in the receiving country to transfer their demand from their home-made goods, to which they are accustomed, to unwonted

[1] Cf. the analysis of ch. II, pp. 29–31.

foreign-made goods of different pattern.[1] Thus the factors in the paying country will have to reduce their rewards more and the price of the output will have to fall more in the case of B than in that of A goods. As against this it must be remarked that the production of B goods is more likely to show decreasing costs over a considerable range, resulting from the larger market.

Thus the burden of an indemnity is twofold. The paying country has to reduce its expenditure by an amount equal to the taxation required to cover the indemnity. In addition it must either allow an unemployment crisis to persist, with the resulting loss of output and income, or it must reduce the real reward to factors of production.

It is sometimes argued that full employment may be maintained without a cut in rewards, owing to the increased purchasing power in the indemnity receiving country operating upon the indemnity paying country's exports. This consideration certainly decreases the severity of the cuts (or of unemployment) suggested as necessary by the previous argument. Only in one condition would the stimulus to purchasing power abroad obviate the necessity for any cuts at all in the indemnity paying country, namely, if the stimulus to employment abroad were so great that the new income receivers, spending no more than a normal fraction of their incomes upon the paying country's goods, which must be supposed to be a small fraction, have so much new income that they buy exports from the paying country equal to the value of the indemnity. Otherwise they will be induced to buy sufficient exports from the paying country to cover the indemnity only by price concessions made by the paying country. But these concessions entail reductions in rewards to factors in the paying country.

§ 4. Capital Movements (preliminary). In considering international capital movements it is necessary to remove the

[1] This will be further accentuated, if the receiving country imposes a a tariff.

simplifying condition that the whole of income is spent. Account must be taken of capital accumulation in the country.

First, income may be classified according to how it arises. Income arises (i) from the production of goods sold to consumers at home, (ii) from the production of goods sold abroad and (iii) from the production of goods which go to swell the stock of capital goods in the country whether fixed or liquid. Incomes derived from foreign investment or by way of indemnity or gift from abroad, as well as profits earned at home and remitted to foreign shareholders or indemnity payments, etc., remitted abroad, are assumed to be nil or to cancel each other exactly in this section. Their effect on the balance was discussed in the foregoing section.

Next, income may be classified according to how it is disposed of. It may be disposed of (i) in the purchase of home-made consumable goods, (ii) in the purchase of imported goods including imported raw materials in home-made goods and (iii) in the form of saving. This accounts for the disposal of the whole of income.

It is convenient to designate the magnitude of income derived from the three aforementioned sources by H, E, and K, namely, income from consumable goods sold in the home market by H, income derived from exports by E, and income derived from additions to capital by K^1; and to designate the *proportion* of income disposed of in the aforementioned ways by h, i and s, namely, proportion of income spent on home-made consumable goods by h, proportion of income spent on imports by i and proportion of income saved by s. Total income is Y. Thus

$$Y = H + E + K = (h + i + s)Y.$$

Also since the amount of income spent on the consumption of home-made goods (excluding imported raw materials) is equal to the amount of income derived from their production

[1] I have used symbols designed to aid the memory of what they stand for. Capital is represented by K (*das Kapital*) instead of C, as C has already been used in the classification into A, B, and C goods (Cf. ch. IV). Capital letters are used for absolute magnitudes and small letters for proportions.

$$hY=H$$
$$\therefore (i+s)Y=E+K.$$

It now no longer follows that $iY=E$, i.e. that there is an exact balance on current account.

The increase in the stock of capital goods in the country is equal to

$$K+Z$$

where Z is the quantity of foreign goods bought not for consumption, but to add to the stock of capital goods.

Total imports being represented by $iY+Z$ and exports by E there is an exact balance of trade, if

$$iY+Z=E.$$

In this condition it is also true that

$$sY=K+Z.$$

We find that Z disappears when the two equations are combined by addition.

Since interest on foreign investments, indemnity payments, etc., are here excluded from consideration, and "goods" are taken to comprise services, the foregoing equation represents an exact balance on current account.

It is not necessary that there should be such an exact balance. If $iY+Z$ is greater than E, there is a passive balance, and conversely.

If there is a passive (or active) balance on current account this must be balanced by a loan from (or to) abroad and/or an outflow (or inflow) of gold. A distinction has to be drawn (cp. Ch. V § 7) between the flows of capital that proceed in quest of profitable investment and those which are the residual effect of an unequal balance of payments.

The international flow of capital is governed by the quest for profit and the conditions of security prevailing. A flow of gold will balance any difference between the totals of current and capital items on the two sides of the account.

It is now required to consider what forces determine (a) the level of employment in the country and (b) the state of the balance of international payments, now that the picture has been complicated.

As before, it will be assumed initially that the rates of efficiency rewards to factors of production expressed in money and the structure of prices in the external world are known and given and also that a gold standard is in operation, so that there are fixed rates of exchange. Assume also that the addition to their stocks of fixed and liquid capital which producers require is known and given. Assume also that the proportion of income which people spend on home-made goods is known and given.

With these assumptions the level of employment in the country may be determined. The technique described in § 2 is used. The relation of the money rates of efficiency rewards of home factors of production to world prices determines the quantity of exports which it will be profitable to make, and the quantity of home produced output required for additions to capital is taken as given. Total income will bear a definite relation to income derived from production for export and from production for capital purposes.

$$(i+s) \, Y = E + K$$

$$\text{or } Y = \frac{1}{i+s}(E+K).$$

This may be alternatively expressed as

$$Y = \frac{1}{1-h}(E+K).$$

This level of income designated by Y, which is related to a definite level of employment and activity, can only be changed if there is a change in the volume of goods which it is profitable to export (E), in the home requirements of capital goods (K) or in the propensity to spend income on home-made consumable goods (h).

The level of employment being so determined, what of the balance of international payments? This is composed of the balance on current account and the balance on capital account.

The former, it has been seen, depends on the relation of $i\text{Y}+\text{Z}$ to E. Assume temporarily that Z is zero.

Now since $i\text{Y}+s\text{Y}=\text{E}+\text{H}$, whether $i\text{Y}$ is greater or less than E, depends on whether the ratio of the proportion of income devoted to imports to the proportion devoted to saving is greater or less than the ratio of income derived from exports to income derived from the production of additions to capital.

There is nothing in the nature of things why these ratios should be equal or why, therefore, there should not be an active or passive balance on current account. This conclusion also follows if Z is not zero.

Let the balance on capital account be wholly governed by the motives of capitalists seeking profit and security and by the policies of official agencies promoting flows of capital for foreign development (but *not* to offset external imbalances of payments).

Let the consequent total balance be active, so that gold flows in.

Questions. Is this inflow likely (i) to affect the level of employment, (ii) to redress the total balance?

In the classical theory of the restorative effect of a gold flow, attention is concentrated on its effect on the current account. In examining that theory, it will be necessary to consider the two questions posed above in conjunction.

§ 5. The Gold Flow and Capital Movements.

Before proceeding with the investigation proposed at the conclusion of the last section it may be expedient to explore the avenue neglected by classical theory and consider the possible direct effect of a gold flow on the capital account, i.e., on the volume of foreign lending or borrowing.

Suppose an active balance on current account not fully counterbalanced by the flow of foreign investment, so that there is a gold inflow.

In this case the amount of saving exceeds the current addition to the stock of capital goods, as may be shown as follows.

By the hypothesis of a favourable balance on current account

$$E > iY + Z.$$

$$\text{But} \quad E + K = iY + sY$$

$$\therefore sY > K + Z.$$

But $K + Z$ is the addition to capital goods at home, comprising those produced abroad as well as at home and sY is the volume of saving.

The excess of saving over the addition to capital goods in the country is equal to the active balance on current account, and this is equal to the net flow of investment abroad, if any, plus the inflow of gold. Thus of the excess of saving part is invested abroad and the residue is invested in the incoming gold.

It makes no difference in this regard whether this gold is held by the banks or in private hands. If it is held by the banks, and they do not make any offsetting or neutralizing operations, bank deposits will be increased by the amount of the gold inflow, and the excess savings of individuals or corporate bodies will take the form of deposits at banks. And if the banks do make offsetting operations, the net effect is still the same; the operations will release a volume of securities equal to the gold inflow and these will be held by the excess savers, while the banks will have a higher proportion of gold and a lower proportion of securities in their list of assets.

As the gold flows in the position inside the country becomes progressively more liquid. If the banks fully offset the inflow, their position becomes progressively more liquid, and if they do not that of the public becomes more liquid. If the banks remain entirely indifferent to their increasing liquidity, then the gold inflow will have no further effect (cf. § 1, (ii)). But there must be a limit to their indifference, especially if the gold is concentrated in the central bank, for ultimately it will own nothing but gold and have no means of earning its livelihood. Conversely if gold flows out the banking system may neutralize the outflow for a time, but if the outflow is persistent they must

10

operate to reinforce its effects—or they will lose all their gold—and thus make the capital position in the country less liquid.

Greater liquidity means that a larger proportion of capital assets consists of gold or deposits at banks, and a smaller proportion of remunerative assets. This situation will tend to reduce short term rates of interest, later long term rates, and finally the yield of securities generally. This, in turn, will tend to make capitalists look about for more lucrative assets; and in looking about, they may look abroad. In the outer world, which has been losing gold, conditions will *pro tanto* be becoming more stringent. The yield of assets will be improving. In consequence it may be expected that an outward flow of investment will be stimulated. The longer the gold flows in, the greater the stimulus. The increased flow of investment abroad will tend to reduce the gold inflow and finally to extinguish it. A new equilibrium may thus be reached.

If the hypothesis of a gold standard is removed, the situation envisaged will lead to a rise of the currency in the foreign exchange market. If the authorities are concerned to preserve some measure of stability, they may buy gold to set a limit to the upward rise, and the same effects as those described in the foregoing paragraph will ensue. And conversely in a condition of weak exchanges.

Even supposing that they set their faces against having any truck with gold, yet if they are influenced by the foreign account at all, the strong condition of the exchanges will make them more ready to expand credit, and, again, the same results will ensue.

This account of the self-righting and ultimately self-eliminating effect of a gold flow seems sensible and in accordance with the facts of former times when capital moved across national frontiers more freely.

The theory is classical in that it postulates a self-righting mechanism at work. It is unclassical in that it attributes the self-righting effect to the capital movements induced and not to a change in the commodity balance (cf. § 1, (iv)). It is possible that this is the most reliable factor in the self-righting mechanism. In that case it is to be expected that in these days, when the international flow of capital in response to the relative yields of securities is much less free than formerly, the self-righting tendencies will not manifest themselves so readily and a progressively less even distribution of gold in the world result.

§ 6. The Gold Flow and the Commodity Balance.

Next consider the effect of a gold inflow on the commodity balance. Commodities are taken, as usual, to include invisible services.

It has been shown (§ 1, (iii)) that gold will operate upon the balance (i) if it raises the total level of production and/or (ii) if it increases the money income distributed per unit of produce, i.e. money costs. It is of the nature of the classical theory to lay greater stress on (ii). The chain of causation which it is necessary to assume between the gold inflow and the rise of money costs has already been explained (§ 1, i–iii).

The primary effect of the gold inflow is to make the economy more liquid. This will tend to stimulate activity, first to the extent that interest rates and the availability of capital for industry are responsive to the greater liquidity—this implies that the banking system does not neutralize the inflow—and, secondly, to the extent that investment is responsive to financial ease. In certain circumstances these responses may not be great.

The increase in investment should lead, through the multiplier, to an increase of activity in the whole economy, notably if there is a slack to be taken up. The increase in activity will be corrective of a favourable balance through its effect in raising Y, and therefore iY, the value of imports on consumption account. It may also lead to an increase in the import of capital goods (Z) to the extent that those undertaking new investment look abroad for part of their capital requirements.

It is not to be expected that the inflow of gold will have an effect on prices or factor rewards unless it does stimulate aggregate demand and activity.   It need not have any marked effect on prices if there is initially considerable unemployment. If employment and profit increase substantially, then a rise of factor rewards is to be expected.

At this point the classical mechanism comes into play.   The higher factor rewards tend, by making home produced goods more expensive, to reduce E, to increase i, and therefore iY, and to increase Z.   These movements are all corrective of the favourable balance.   It is to be noted, however, that they all tend to have a damping effect on activity—the reduction of exports and the increase in the propensity to import both consumer goods and capital goods.   Since, however, these changes in E, iY and Z all flow from the increase in aggregate demand and activity, their damping effect on activity must, by ordinary supply and demand principles,[1] be less than the initial increase in activity caused by the gold inflow.   Thus the net effect of the gold inflow must be corrective.   Similar reasonings would show that the effect of an outflow would tend to be corrective of an unfavourable balance.

If there is initially full employment, the increase of liquidity, if not counteracted, will still have some effect in stimulating investment.   The extra demand will tend to raise prices and factor rewards and so exert the corrective effects, already described, on the balance.   Modern experience suggests that stress should also be placed on the tendency of the excess of aggregate demand over the supply potential to result in waiting lists and a longer time interval between orders and delivery. These, no less than price increases, will tend to reduce the flow of exports and to increase the flow of imports.

Thus the classical theory of the curative effect of a gold flow need not be challenged in principle.   But it will only have this effect if counteracting measures are not adopted to prevent an increase of liquidity outside the banking system.   And it may only have an appreciable effect, if the banking system actively co-operates by causing an expansion of credit, on its larger gold base, of sizable proportions.   Furthermore the setting

[1] Cf. H. D. Henderson, *Supply & Demand*, p. 27.

must be right. The supply of capital for investment, as symbolized by a fall in interest rates, must be responsive to the greater liquidity, and investment itself must be responsive to greater financial ease.

The fault in the gold flow theory does not lie in the general principles. Rather the question may be raised whether the influence of the gold flow is important enough to do the work required of it in a reasonably short time. In the kind of classical theory here set forth the gold flow was represented as the sole influence operating through the balance of payments that tended to make the balance improve or worsen. If there are other influences also operating through the foreign trade relations, it may happen that these are more powerful, and are sufficient to offset and reverse such influence as the gold flow has.

§ 7. Volume of Exports v. Excess of Exports.

So far we have seen that an inflow of gold will, neglecting its effect on international capital movements, only serve to redress the balance of trade, if and in so far as it stimulates demand in the receiving country. A view is thus presented of foreign influence sometimes working, through an inflow of gold, to stimulate output in a country, until a new equilibrium is reached, and sometimes working, through an outflow, to depress output. If the view is extended to include the world as a whole, but confined to a single period of time, there results a picture of some countries being stimulated to expansion by foreign influence while others are induced by foreign influence to contract; for at any time inflows of gold in some countries are exactly balanced by outflows from others.

Now this picture singularly misrepresents the true state of affairs. The trade cycle has usually been in the past, notably when the gold standard was operating smoothly, a world-wide phenomenon, the phases of which have tended to occur, if not simultaneously, at least in fairly rapid succession in different countries. A set-back to prosperity may occur in one important country or group of countries, but sooner or later all or most of the others are drawn into the maelstrom by forces which can only be supposed to operate through those trading relations of which the international balance of payments gives a summary. It is hardly likely that each of a large number of countries would, if they were all entirely insulated from one another, share to anything like the extent they have in fact shared in the common world prosperity or adversity. And so it becomes necessary to suppose that in the downward phase there is somehow transmitted through their international trading relations an adverse force affecting all or most countries simultaneously; and conversely in the revival. This is a very different state of affairs from that suggested by the view that the stimulating or depressing effect of foreign transactions is channelled through a gold flow, which, in so far as it is stimulating or depressing, must simultaneously be exerting an equal and opposite influence in different countries at the same time.[1]

The analysis already given in Chapter VI, § 2, points to the correct view. There the direct influence of the volume, as distinct from the excess, of exports, was analysed. If the income which a country is able to earn by its exports increases, the income and activity of the country as a whole is stimulated, and conversely. Thus it may happen that falling exports so depress the level of activity, including investment activity, in a country that imports fall still more, so that an inflow of gold occurs; but the depressing effect of the falling volume of exports outweighs any stimulating effect which the inflow of gold may exert. This, indeed, is what must be supposed to happen to a number of countries in the downward phase of the trade cycle.

The world diffusion of a depression may be set forth as follows. A point comes at which the factors making for recession in the world as a whole become stronger than those making for continued advance. This tends to weaken the world-price level or the state of world demand. Each and

[1] I owe appreciation of the cardinal importance of this argument to the persistence of my former pupil, Mr. S. D. Pollard.

every country, including those which are not themselves the theatre of the triumph of adverse forces, finds that the volume of A and B goods, which it can export at a profit, is reduced. Thus each and every country is subjected to an adverse influence through the fall of exports, and conversely in a revival. This is independent of its net balance of payments.

It should be noted that each separate country may be deceived into taking a wrong view of the causes of depressions, attributing them to failures of the export market. This may be a true view of the channel through which the depressing force operates upon it. But it was necessary to assume in the foregoing argument that there was a balance of forces making for depression in the world as a whole, *other* than those connected with foreign trade. For when the economy of the world as a whole is considered there are no exports and imports! All trade is internal trade. Even those countries which are the seat of the trouble may take a wrong view, since the effect of the weakening in the world position will react back upon their exports, and the evil of falling exports may be more plainly visible than the true causes of the trouble.

Countries which in these circumstances develop a passive balance may be deceived even as to the nature of the *impact* of the depression upon them, wrongly attributing more importance to the passive balance than to the falling volume of exports.

If, then, the gold flow is not the predominating foreign influence on the level of a country's activity, and if, as was shown in Chapter VI, § 6, a gold flow can only bring foreign trade to balance by its influence on the level of a country's activity, it follows that the gold flow cannot be regarded as a reliable instrument for bringing foreign trade to balance. This argument as to the ineffectiveness of the gold flow is independent of what the authorities may do in the way of "monkeying about" with the gold; it would hold, if they allowed and assisted it to exert a large effect on the quantity of money in the country. The argument may indeed justify the authorities in their monkeying about; for if the alleged curative effect of the gold flow on the balance is unimportant, they may sometimes be justified in impeding its influence on the internal monetary system if they have other good reasons for desiring to do so.

The foregoing argument does not derogate from the possible influence of the gold flow on the balance of payments through its influence on international capital movements. (Cf. § 5.) But in a world in which international capital movements are themselves obstructed for other reasons, this influence is likely to be frustrated; so once again the authorities are justified in dealing with the gold in the way best adapted to the internal situation.

It is to be noted that emphasis on gold movements not only gives a wrong idea of the influence of foreign trading relations on the level of activity, but also provides a bad criterion for monetary policy. When forces making for depression in the world overcome those making for continued expansion and the world enters upon the downward spin, it is desirable that each country should assist to the best of its abilities to stimulate revival. But if each country guides its monetary policy of expansion or contraction by reference to the balance of payments, some will pursue an expansive and others a restrictive policy. There will be no net balance of expansive policy and no net monetary effort in the world as a whole towards revival.

§ **8. Summary.** (i) A classical theory of the balance has been stated in which the gold flow is held automatically to secure an even balance. The assumptions required by this theory have been enumerated. Its main defect is that it does not deal systematically with the level of employment.

(ii) By means of the multiplier analysis, it is shown that if people spend the whole of their incomes, a balance will occur automatically without the intervention of a gold flow (a) when current exchange of goods and services only are taken into account and (b) when interest, dividends, donations, and indemnity payments are also brought in. A full level of employment is not automatically secured; this depends on efficiency rewards to factors being at the right level in relation to world prices.

(iii) When the accumulation and movement of capital are taken into account, it is shown that payments do not balance automatically. The multiplier method is extended to cover this case, and it is again shown that the level of employment depends on the relation of efficiency rewards of factors to world prices.

(iv) The gold flow may be expected to tend to even out a balance by influencing relative liquidity and the yield of assets in different countries and so producing a compensatory international movement of capital, provided that such movement is comparatively easy.

(v) The influence of a gold flow on the balance on current account is examined, having regard to its possible influence on (a) the level of activity and (b) money costs of production. It is shown that it can only exert a self-adjusting influence via (b) if it has an antecedent and greater influence on the level of activity (a).

(vi) The gold flow theory concentrates attention on surpluses (or deficiencies) in the external balance of payments. But a change in the value of exports may have a greater effect on the level of activity in a country than an excess or deficiency. This throws doubt on the reliability of the gold flow as a mechanism for restoring an external balance to equilibrium.

CHAPTER VII

CORRECTING AN IMBALANCE

§ **1. Fundamental Principles.** It may be expedient to make a fresh start and approach the theory of the balance of payments by considering what should be done, in various circumstances, to deal with a balance that is out of equilibrium, or, to use a convenient modern term, to correct an "imbalance".

For this purpose it is desirable to bring the theory of employment into relation with the theory of the external balance. The question of employment has already cropped up in a number of connexions. In Ch. IV, § 6, it was explained that if rewards (other than profit) were set at too high a level in relation to a country's average efficiency, this would cause unemployment. In Ch. VI, § 1, it was explained how the classical theory assumed full employment, and would suffice to yield a precise determination of foreign exchange equilibrium with freely floating exchanges, only if full employment was assumed. Later in Ch. VI it was again shown how, if rewards to factors were above a certain level, unemployment would be caused.

In what follows it is assumed that the objective of policy is not only to get an equal balance of external payments, but also at the same time to maintain full employment at home. We are not concerned with the precise definition of this expression.

The basic equations set forth in Ch. VI, § 4, will serve us, but certain new terms are needed. First let Y^s be the level of income that is achieved when there is full employment, however that rather vexed expression be defined. It will be convenient sometimes to refer to Y^s as the "supply potential", since it stands for the total value of all the goods that can be produced when the productive resources of the community

140

are fully engaged. Since the classical assumption of full employment is dropped, we can say that

$$Y = H + E + K = (h+i+s)\, Y = \text{or} < Y^s.$$

Where the sum of the three demands is tending to run above the supply potential, we have inflationary pressure. The excess of total demand over the supply potential may be called the "inflationary gap". Then one or both of two things can happen. Take them one at a time. Prices may rise at once so as to reduce demand to the supply potential. The high prices may reduce the demand coming from abroad (E). The ordinary consumer will find that his income will not go so far while the high prices bring inflationary profits to producers; the combined effect of this is to reduce the proportion of income consumed (h) while raising the proportion saved (s), the extra saving being done out of the inflated profits. This reduces consumption (H), but, by itself, has no effect on investment (K). Thus the net effect is a reduction in aggregate demand. If this were the sole effect of the initial excess of aggregate demand, we should have a new temporary equilibrium, at a higher price level, which could be described as

$$Y = H + E + K = (h+i+s)\, Y = Y^s.$$

But it is possible, and, in many circumstances probable, that prices will not rise so much, and that the aggregate demand will continue to exceed the supply potential. This excess may be called the quantum of unfulfilled orders. To describe this condition, we shall write Y^d for aggregate demand and H^d, E^d, and K^d for the demand for goods (and services) for home consumption, the demand for exports and the demand for goods on capital account respectively. H^d being the demand for consumption goods and H the income flowing by the supply of consumption goods, $(H^d - H)$ is the quantum of unfulfilled orders (or waiting list) on consumption account; similarly with the other items. We can now describe the condition in which aggregate demand exceeds the supply potential as follows:

$$Y^d = H^d + E^d + K^d > H + E + K$$
$$> (h + i + s)Y$$
$$> Y^s.$$

In this, or any other, condition of disequilibrium it remains true that

$$Y = H + E + K = (h + i + s)Y.$$

In equilibrium $Y^d = Y^s$, while there is disequilibrium if

$$Y^d > \text{ or } < Y^s.$$

In the case where aggregate demand (Y^d) is less than the supply potential (Y^s), realized income (Y) is also less than the supply potential or full employment income (Y^s).

We must now look to the subdivision of demand. Whether the above equilibrium ($Y^d = Y^s$) obtains or not, it remains true that income flowing from the sale of goods and services at home is equal to income spent upon them, i.e. $H = hY$. Therefore

$$E + K = (i + s) \ Y.$$

It is also true that whether the above equilibrium ($Y^d = Y^s$) obtains or not, there can be the following possibilities:

$$E > \text{ or} = \text{ or } < iY + Z.$$

For the purpose of this exposition we may assume that there are no gifts and that there is no spontaneous movement of capital into or out of the country, or, alternatively, that the spontaneous movements that occur cancel each other out, and that all the net movement of capital that occurs is the *result* of an imbalance of all other payments and therefore calls for correction.

If exports (E) are not equal to imports ($iY + Z$), we say that there is an external disequilibrium, or imbalance. If there is this kind of disequilibrium, it follows necessarily that there is also a disequilibrium between domestic saving and domestic investment. If there is an excess of exports over imports, there is also necessarily an excess of saving over domestic investment. This may be written,

$$E - (iY + Z) = sY - (K + Z).$$

We should not call the imbalance of external payments and the imbalance between saving and investment two *kinds* of disequilibrium, for they are indissolubly linked together and are the mirror images of each other.

But the employment disequilibrium, viz. $Y^d \neq Y^s$, is entirely different. There may be an employment disequilibrium whether in the form of inflation or unemployment ($Y^d > Y^s$ or $Y^d < Y^s$), while there is a perfectly equal external balance of payments. Or there may be an unequal external balance, even though the internal economy is well balanced, in the sense of suffering neither from inflation nor depression ($Y^d = Y^s$). The correct remedy for one kind of imbalance cannot be gauged without reference to whether the other kind of imbalance is also present, and, if so, in what form.

If $Y^d = Y^s$ and $iY + Z = E$, the economy is in equilibrium in both respects. We shall next set out four combinations of imbalance.

1. $Y^d < Y^s$ and $iY + Z < E$
2. $Y^d > Y^s$ and $iY + Z > E$
3. $Y^d < Y^s$ and $iY + Z > E$
4. $Y^d > Y^s$ and $iY + Z < E$

(i) In the first of these situations there is unemployment and an external surplus. The correct remedy for such a case is not in doubt: it is expansion. It may be more explicit and memorable to write, instead of "expansion", the word "inflation". But that word has become odious since the second war, as indeed it was at an earlier period, because there have been few, if any, occasions when inflation was required as a remedy, and much inflation that has been harmful and even pernicious. "Reflation"[1] can be used.

[1] The word reflation was coined at a time, after the onset of the great depression of 1929–32, to avoid the odium of "inflation", when inflation was desirable, just as "disinflation" has recently been coined to avoid the use of "deflation", which became odious between the wars. "Reflation" and "disinflation", should not, however, be regarded as wholly evasive terms. Reflation carries the sense of restoring the situation after a previous excess of deflation, and disinflation that of restoring the situation after a previous excess of inflation, and in those contexts it is perfectly proper to use them.

Reflation (or expansionist measures) will have the effect of increasing investment (K), and thereby income (Y), and thereby imports on consumer account (iY) and perhaps also imports of capital goods (Z). It will thus have the joint effect of increasing income and employment and of reducing the favourable balance, being therefore what is required to rectify both the prevailing disequilibria. The classic case in which these symptoms were jointly present and in which accordingly reflation was plainly desirable was that of the United States after the Great Depression. She had intense domestic unemployment and a favourable balance. Thus the expansionist tendency of the New Deal, to whatever criticisms particular features of it are open, was on the right lines.

This corrective is partly in line with classical thinking, partly not. According to that thinking the inflow of gold, due to the favourable balance, was expected to exert an inflationary effect inside the country. Extremists may have held that the mere inflow would suffice to produce a sufficient inflation to correct the favourable balance, but it would be entirely in line anyhow with later classical doctrine to suppose that the banking system must co-operate actively by bringing about an expansion of currency notes and of banking deposits fully in proportion to the accession of gold. More modern thinking has held that even this would not necessarily bring about sufficient reflation; easy credit might not stimulate activity sufficiently to restore full employment and make imports rise up to match exports; you can bring a horse to the water but you cannot make it drink.

Accordingly it has been urged that in these conditions easy credit should be supplemented by public works constituting a direct supplement to the volume of investment (K). It was also urged by some, who were in doubt whether useful public works had sufficient scope, that the investments of certain industries, which were heavy capital users, should be planned in advance and expedited or enlarged, when the conditions now under discussion were present. This did not necessarily imply a "nationalization" of those industries, but the argu-

ment that by this means the public authorities would obtain
control over a large range of investment was placed in the
foreground by those who recommended nationalization.[1]
What is called fiscal policy has also been brought into consideration; it has been held that governmental authorities,
central or local, should reduce their sinking funds or even run
deficits in such a situation.   This would reduce the propensity
to save (s) and thereby have the same effect on the two disequilibria as an increase of investment (K).   All these lines of
thought are directed to supplementing and enlarging the
inflation presumed to occur as a consequence of the gold
inflow.

But there is one respect in which this thinking goes in the
opposite direction to classical doctrine. It relies on the
increase in investment (K), possibly conjoined with a decreased
propensity to save (s), to stimulate general activity (Y), and
so redress unemployment, and on the increase in income (Y)
and therefore in imports (iY), and possibly in the purchase of
capital goods abroad (Z) to rectify the external imbalance.   No
reference has been made to any rise of prices or factor rewards,
on which the classical theory relied for the correction of the
external imbalance.   Such rises may indeed occur, but from
the modern point of view, so far from contributing to the
successful issue, they are decidedly unhelpful in these circumstances.   The classical doctrine relies on the increase of
prices and factor rewards to tend to reduce exports (E) and
to increase the propensity to import (i)—because home-made
goods become more expensive—and thereby to increase
imports (iY).   The modern view does not look to correction

[1] Nationalization has not so far worked quite like this in Britain since
the second war. By this argument the nationalized industries should
have retarded and reduced their programmes when the country was
suffering from strong inflationary pressure.   But they have argued that
their capital programmes were too important to be interfered with.
Indeed from the point of view of inflation and depression the situation
seems to have been made worse, rather than better, by nationalization,
since this group of important industries has been taken out of the sphere
of influence of banking policy, whether of credit ease or tightness.   However, later on this position may be reconsidered and altered.

of the external imbalance through a decline of exports (E)—
to the extent that this occurred it would be considered undesirable—but solely to a rise of imports ($iY+Z$), and it looks
to that rise, not because of any increase in the propensity
to import (i), but because of the higher level of income (Y).
To put the matter briefly, both views expect a rise in imports
(iY), but whereas the classical doctrine expected that through
a rise in i (assuming Y constant) the modern view seeks it
through a rise in Y (hoping that i will *not* rise).   All this applies
only to the first combination of disequilibria, which we are
now examining.

Whereas on the classical view the decline in exports (E) and
the rise of the propensity to import (i) are of the essence, the
modern view is bound to recognize that there may be some
such effects—owing to the rise in domestic prices and factor
rewards—but regards them as unfortunate by-products, to be
avoided if possible.   The reason for this is plain.   One of the
two disequilibria to be corrected in the situation we are
examining is domestic unemployment.   A fall of exports
owing to higher prices quoted by home producers or a turning
away of home consumers from home-made to foreign goods
for the same reason will both tend to exacerbate unemployment at home, which is one of the two evils that requires to
be cured.   Thus, to revert to our former illustration, if the
expansionist policy in the U.S. in the 'thirties had been more
powerful than it was, it would by no means have been helpful
if it had caused a loss of her export trade or caused her
consumers to turn away from American towards foreign
goods, because both those effects would have tended to
increase her own unemployment, which was already so severe.
The object of an expansionist policy in these conditions is to
get the greatest possible increase of activity with the minimum
rise in prices or factor rewards.

(ii) The second condition to be considered is where there is
inflationary pressure at home ($Y^d > Y^s$) and an external deficit.
Here both disequilibria require the remedy of deflation.   This
was the prevailing condition in most countries, except the

United States, for most of the time during the decade after the second war. Deflation tends to reduce investment (K), possibly to increase the propensity to save (s), and so to bring aggregate demand (Y^d) down to the supply potential (Y^s).

Both the disequilibria that we are now examining are opposite to those considered under (i). Unhappily, it is not possible to use converse language throughout, owing to the fact that an excess of demand (Y^d) over the supply potential (Y^s) is not symmetrically opposed to a deficiency of demand. In the latter case part of the supply potential goes out of work; but in the former case it is not possible to employ more resources than are available for employment, so that income cannot actually rise above the Y^s level. Where Y^d exceeds Y^s, the difference takes one of two forms, a rise of prices over costs or a quantum of unfulfilled orders. It is the latter of these conditions which has been especially prominent during periods of inflationary pressure after the second war.

As deflation reduces the excess of aggregate demand over the supply potential, it will bring down prices and reduce the quantum of unfulfilled orders. This will have the effect of increasing exports (E) and reducing the propensity to import (i), and thereby imports (iY), and so correct the unfavourable balance of trade.

It is to be observed that the action of disinflation accords more closely with classical ideas than that of reflation. The reason for this is easy to see. Because they assumed full employment, it was impossible for them to get a correct view of the operation of reflation upon an under-employed economy: by assuming full employment, they failed to observe that, when demand was insufficient, there would be unemployment. But the assumption of full employment does not lead to a corresponding error on the other side of the fence. Whereas, when demand is insufficient to give employment to all available resources, less than all available resources will be employed, when demand is sufficient to give employment to more than all the available resources, more than all the available resources cannot be employed. In fine the classical assumption

11

of full employment is correct on the other side of the fence. So, when reflation is introduced into an under-employed economy, it causes more resources to come into employment; but when disinflation is introduced into an economy where aggregate demand exceeds the supply potential, it does not necessarily cause people to go out of employment—provided, that is, that it is confined to what is needed to lop off the excess of the demand over the supply potential.

And so, while we expect reflation to correct a favourable balance through its effect on the general level of real income (Y), and so on imports (iY), we cannot expect disinflation, provided that it is limited as already described, to cure an unfavourable balance through its effect on the general level of real income (Y), since, when thus limited, it will have no such effect. And so we are driven back to the classical mechanism. Disinflation will cure the external imbalance by operating on exports (E) and on the propensity to import (i), and thereby on imports (iY). By reducing the "inflationary gap" it will bring down any excess of prices over costs (including normal profits) and so make the domestic prices both of export goods and goods competing with foreign imports, more favourable relatively to foreign prices, and it will reduce the quantum of unfulfilled orders. The latter of these effects is important. Inability to deliver promptly alienates foreign customers, thus reducing exports, and drives home customers to supply their needs from abroad, thus increasing imports. Thus the restoration of prompt delivery can have an important effect in correcting an external imbalance.

Variations in the quantum of unfulfilled orders have not in the past figured prominently in economic theory; they are likely to do so in future. These are the analogue on the inflationary side to the variations of employment on the deflationary side which Lord Keynes brought into prominence in economic doctrine. Classical theory tended to hold that variations in the flow of monetary demand acted wholly on the price level, both upwards and downwards. Keynes discredited this doctrine in its relation to a fall in monetary demand, by stressing its effect in producing unemployment, rather than and instead of a commensurate fall in prices; and this created a considerable re-orientation of economic thought.   In future the effect of a rise in monetary demand in causing an increase in the quantum of unfulfilled orders, rather than and instead of a commensurate rise in prices, is likely to be deemed of no less importance, and should create a re-orientation of thinking about inflation analagous to Keynes's re-orientation in regard to deflation and depression.

(iii) The third case for study is that of a country suffering from unemployment and an external deficit, thus being doubly misfortunate. This differs markedly from the case just considered where the combination of internal inflationary pressure, and external deficit called clearly for the policy of deflation. Where there is domestic unemployment, deflation is entirely out of place, since it would render the unemployment more severe. This situation occurred in a number of countries before 1939 and was prominently in the minds of those who were responsible for plans for post-war reconstruction, to be discussed in the next chapter.

The domestic unemployment seems to call for a stimulation of investment (K) and possibly a depression of the propensity to save (s), on the lines of (i) above.   But such a policy would aggravate the external imbalance. It is desirable to increase aggregate demand (Y^d); but in these circumstances this must be done, not by increasing K and reducing s, which would make the external imbalance still worse, but by increasing E and reducing i, and, possibly, Z. This is the case referred to in Ch. IV § 6, where the level of domestic factor rewards was specified as too high in relation to their efficiency and the world price level.

What accordingly is required is a reduction of factor rewards. This would, subject to limitations to be discussed below, tend to increase exports (E) and to reduce the propensity to import (i), by reducing the domestic prices at which home goods could be quoted, whether for export or the home market, relatively to foreign prices for the same goods. This would rectify the external imbalance and also improve domestic employment, thus redressing both disequilibria. The reduction in factor rewards is a more radical remedy than the reduction of prices by the mere skimming off of inflationary profit (excess of prices over costs) discussed under (ii) above. If the situation is one of unemployment, and not of inflationary pressure, there is not likely to be any excess of profit available to be skimmed off; profits are likely to be depressed. In this situation an improvement in the external balance, which is required, can be secured only by a reduction of costs. Of course the remedy of deflation applied under (ii) above might reduce demand below the level of the supply potential and still not suffice to correct the external imbalance fully. The situation (ii) would at that point be transformed into situation (iii), which we are now discussing.

According to classical theory a reduction in costs would come about automatically in consequence of a gold outflow, or of a gold outflow accompanied by a commensurate restriction of bank credit. Doubt has been thrown on whether things are likely so to work out in practice. It is sometimes said that factor rewards are more resistant to reductions now than they were when the classical theory was formulated. It is doubtful, however, if they were ever readily amenable to reductions. Modern writers have stressed that, if we are realistic, we should not expect any notable downward reductions of factor rewards to occur, and search has accordingly been made for other methods of redressing a situation of this type.

The search for an alternative remedy, however, should not be regarded as a mere policy of defeatism, and of appeasement towards perversely recalcitrant wage or salary earners. There are reasons of equity, as well as of expediency, for not seeking redress by a reduction of wages and salaries. The victims may feel that the depression of rewards to which it is proposed to subject them ought to be, but may not in fact be, shared by those who enjoy a fixed income from property and by profit takers. Furthermore, a move to reduce wages may not be widely diffused, but may fall with especially severe and inequitable incidence on those in "unsheltered" occupations. In most free economies wages and salaries are regulated by separate bargains in the various industries or crafts. Some advocate a national "wage policy" whereby wages throughout an economy would be decreased (or increased) on a uniform plan, as the occasion required. Experience does not suggest that such a policy would make an all-round reduction of wages easier. Occasions when that happened, such as that of the Premiers' Plan in Australia in 1930, have been rare exceptions.

In face of these difficulties it has been suggested that the appropriate remedy for this type of situation is a devaluation of the currency. This secures a widespread and uniform reduction of real incomes. Money rewards to factors having become too high in relation to the world price level, it is suggested that the logical and appropriate adjustment is to alter the rate at which the domestic currency exchanges for currencies in the outer world. It may be objected that this is an obnoxious sleight of hand for evading the resistance of earners to having their rewards reduced. However, if it is in fact the case that it is better for all to accept some reduction of pay rather than have continuing unemployment, the expedient may be justifiable. Particular groups of wage or salary earners have the satisfaction of knowing that under this method the sacrifice due to the depreciated value of the currency is widely spread over all classes of income receivers. It must be noted that in the situation now under discussion in which money rewards are too high in relation to the productive efficiency of the country, there is no way whatever of securing full employment save by getting a reduction of real rewards— unless of course some foreign country feels inclined to make continuing gifts to the country in question.

The remedy of devaluation has come into the foreground of discussion during the last thirty years. It is subject to certain limitations discussed in the next section.

(iv) Finally we come to the case where there is internal inflationary pressure accompanied by a favourable external balance. The United States has been in this position for periods since the second war. Germany was so in 1956. The internal situation seems to call for deflation, but this would tend to increase the external imbalance. If the internal inflationary pressure is strong, some measure of deflation may be needed in any case. The fact remains that it tends to exacerbate the external disequilibrium. By parity of reasoning to that of the last paragraph an *upward* valuation of the currency is called for, or, alternatively, an upward revision of factor rewards. Since it is so much easier to obtain an upward revision than a downward revision in these, the expedient of upward currency revaluation does not have to be considered so seriously in this case. An upward revaluation of the German mark was proposed in 1956, but the authorities foresaw so many wage increases coming along, that they felt that, even if at the moment German factor rewards were too low in relation to German efficiency and the world price level, that situation would soon correct itself in the natural course.

It may be well to re-state the alternatives set out on p. 143 and add examples and the remedies which, subject to qualifications, may be deemed appropriate.

	Examples	*Remedies*
1. $Y^d < Y^s$ and $iY + Z < E$	U.S. 1931–1939.	Reflate.
2. $Y^d > Y^s$ and $iY + Z > E$	European countries 1946–1952.	Disinflate.
3. $Y^d < Y^s$ and $iY + Z > E$	Many countries 1931.	Reduce factor rewards or devalue currency.
4. $Y^d > Y^s$ and $iY + Z < E$	U.S. for parts of period 1946–1956. Germany 1956.	Increase factor rewards or revalue currency upwards.

These "remedies" may, however, need modification when we take into account the maxims of good-neighbourliness. (Ch. VIII, § 1.)

§ 2. Reduction of Factor Rewards and Elasticity of Demand.

Warning was given in the last section that the doctrine that a reduction of factor rewards would improve the external balance by stimulating exports and reducing the propensity to import, might be subject to limitations. It has been pointed out by some authors that the improvement in the balance will only occur if the elasticity of demand is sufficient. For, while the offer of goods at lower prices will indubitably tend to increase the volume of exports, it will only increase the total value of the country's exports if the expansion in volume is proportionately greater than the reduction in the prices at which it offers them, that is if the elasticity of demand for them is greater than one. Otherwise the total value of exports will fall. The reduction of domestic supply prices will indubitably tend to reduce both the volume and price per unit, and therefore the total value, of imports. But the saving in expenditure on imports may in certain circumstances be insufficient to offset the loss of revenue from exports.

This line of thought goes counter to the more general principles set out in Ch. IV, § 6. It was there assumed that the law of comparative costs is translated into a relative price structure giving the right motivation to private traders, by the rewards to factors in each country being fixed at levels which are proportional to their average efficiency, relatively to that in other countries. If unemployment and an adverse external balance occur, this seems to point unequivocally to the rewards having been set at too high a level at home in relation to efficiency. The country will not be exporting all the goods in which it has a comparative advantage and may even import some in which it has that advantage. Thus a reduction of rewards seems clearly called for.

It is to be observed that while the doctrine of insufficient elasticity has been used particularly to cast doubt on the curative effect of a devaluation, it applies with equal force to a direct reduction of money rewards to factors. And it has a more far-reaching and alarming corollary. It has been a background assumption throughout our discussion of foreign trade that a country is well advised to seek every day and in every way to raise the efficiency of her production. But this doctrine of insufficient elasticity implies that a country would *injure* her external balance by raising her efficiency—unless she was most careful to *prevent* her improved efficiency being reflected in lower prices.[1] While we must by no means rule out the possibility of insufficient elasticity, one would expect it to be the exceptional case in the normal run of development. But one should be very wary of assuming that the elasticities will be sufficient, where the opening position is one of very large maladjustment, such as may occur after a great war.

A formula may be supplied. Let x stand for the price level of exports prior to the reduction of factor rewards and let x also stand for the volume of exports prior to that reduction, so that $x \times x$ stands for the value of total exports. Let rewards be reduced so as to permit a reduction in the prices asked for exports by one point $(= \frac{1}{x}$ of the previous price level). The increase in the volume of exports will then be ε_{fd}, where this term stands for the elasticity of foreign demand for exports. Owing to the notation chosen, all four elasticities referred to below (each represented by ε) reduce simply to the amount by which demand or supply changes in response to a change of price of 1 unit. Let the elasticity of the home supply of exports be infinite; this is not unrealistic if the experiment is carried out (as it should be) only when there is initially unemployment. The loss of money due to the reduction by one point in prices charged for the pre-existing flow of exports is x (i.e. $1 \times x$ units of exports); the gain of money due to the extra exports is $(x-1) \times \varepsilon_{fd}$. Therefore the net gain is

$$\varepsilon_{fd} (x-1) - x.$$

This is positive if

$$\varepsilon_{fd} > \frac{x}{x-1}.$$

In similar manner let the price level and volume of imports each be represented by x, making the total value of imports equal to $x \times x$. This would be correct, if trade was initially in

[1] Cf. Professor Sir Dennis Robertson, *Economic Journal*, December 1945, p. 325.

equal balance. Suppose the elasticity of the foreign supply of imports to be initially infinite. A general drop in domestic prices of one point, while foreign prices remain the same, may be taken to have the same effect on the home demand for foreign goods as a rise in foreign prices by one point, home prices remaining the same. (If one substituted a devaluation of the currency for an all round reduction in factor rewards, foreign prices would actually rise by one point when expressed in domestic currency, retaining the assumption of infinite elasticity of foreign supply.) If ε_{hd} stands for the elasticity of home demand for foreign goods, then $\varepsilon_{hd} \times x$ will be the reduction in the money spent on imports.

The reduction of domestic rewards will give a net gain on the foreign balance if

$$\varepsilon_{fd}\left(\frac{x-1}{x}\right)+\varepsilon_{hd}>1.$$

If initially trade is not in balance, but the value of imports exceeds the value of exports, as it is reasonable to suppose in this consideration of a measure designed to cure an imbalance, we may suppose the value of imports to be equal to $y(x \times x)$, where $y>1$. As our units are chosen entirely for convenience, we may suppose the value of imports $y(x \times x)$ to consist of yx units of imports at the price level x. In these conditions the reduction of quoted prices will cause an improvement in the balance, if

$$\varepsilon_{fd}\left(\frac{x-1}{x}\right)+y\varepsilon_{hd}>1.$$

If the supply of imports has not infinite elasticity, the formula is more complicated, but it is likely to give a value not far removed from the simple formula.[1]

These elasticities are notoriously difficult to evaluate in practice. Some statistical calculations have suggested rather

[1] If ϵ_{fs} is the elasticity of the foreign supply of imports, the gain on the side of imports is:

$$\frac{x \cdot \epsilon_{hd}\,(\epsilon_{fs}+1)}{\epsilon_{hd}+\epsilon_{fs}} - \frac{\epsilon_{hd}^2 \cdot \epsilon_{fs}}{(\epsilon_{fs}+\epsilon_{hd})^2}.$$

low values for them. A point of cardinal importance is that, wherever competition is imperfect, the effect of a reduced price quotation on the volume of sales is likely to be rather slow-working. This means that the short effect is likely to be less than the longer-run effect. The corollary is that a reduction of factor rewards (or, its equivalent in this connexion, a devaluation) is not likely to be a good weapon for dealing with a transitory imbalance, but more likely to be an effective remedy for one that seems likely to be long lasting, sometimes called a "fundamental disequilibrium".

The question of the merits of devaluation has been much perplexed by the ill-starred devaluation of sterling in 1949. Two conditions were wrong for that experiment.

1. The case of Britain in that year belongs to the second, and not the third, of the cases analysed above.[1] Aggregate demand was running very much in excess of the supply potential and the devaluation served to exacerbate that condition. Deflation was the appropriate remedy at that time. Indeed it can be argued that the most elementary condition for a devaluation was not present, since Britain's balance of external payments on current account was not adverse in 1949 and had not been in 1948. There was an adverse tendency in the months immediately preceding the devaluation, but that was due to the speculative anticipation of this remedy, which was strongly urged in the United States in the early months of 1949.

2. It has been seen that devaluation should normally have a twofold effect, namely on exports and imports. It cannot be said that it will inevitably have the effect of increasing the value of exports as measured in foreign currency (although it will increase their volume) and it may well decrease their value; but this should normally be more than offset by the decline in expenditure, again expressed in foreign currency, on imports. But in 1949 British imports were subject to strong direct controls; the marginal buyers of imports were not allowed by law to buy them; consequently it was not to be expected that a rise in their prices expressed in sterling would

[1] See pp. 146-149.

have the effect of reducing the amount of them purchased; and it did not do so.

In these circumstances the devaluation did not have any good effect on the balance of payments, but it had a bad one on the domestic side, by increasing both the inflationary gap (owing to the enlarged volume of exports) and the level of import prices, which in turn led to a spiral between wages and prices. No lesson can be drawn for the worth of devaluation as a remedy in appropriate circumstances, from the experience of its use on this unfortunate occasion.[1]

A word may be said here on the effects of devaluation on the "terms of trade". It is sometimes supposed that it tends to worsen them; indeed a devaluation is sometimes represented as a method of trying to rectify an imbalance by offering to the outside world the exports of a country at a lower rate in terms of the imports it buys. This is not so. A country does indeed, by devaluation, try to push more of its exports upon the outer world; but simultaneously it seeks to deter its citizens from buying so many imports from the outer world. Both these procedures tend to have a lowering effect on prices outside; there is no *a priori* presumption that the devaluation will have a greater effect in lowering the prices, expressed in foreign currency, that it asks for its exports than in lowering the prices, again expressed in foreign currency, that it has to pay for its imports. The country's terms of trade will be worsened or improved according as whether

$$\frac{\varepsilon_{hs}}{\varepsilon_{hs}+\varepsilon_{fd}} > \quad \text{or} \quad < \frac{\varepsilon_{hd}}{\varepsilon_{fs}+\varepsilon_{hd}}.$$

Which condition will obtain depends on the particular circumstances of the case.

In the elasticity formula for the trade balance no account is taken of the "multiplier" effect of devaluation on internal activity and income. If the effect on the balance, prior to taking the multiplier effect into account, is favourable, then it

[1] It is sometimes urged that the devaluation of sterling in 1949 had a rectifying effect on the balance of payments of the outer sterling area; but this is extremely doubtful.

will be favourable after taking that into account also, although not in so great a degree.   This assumes that the level of investment and the propensity to save are unaffected by the change.[1]

But what happens if the increase in exports has an effect on investment?

§ 3. Growth and the Balance of Trade.

It was stated in Ch. VI, § 7, that a fall in a country's export outlets might "so depress the level of activity, including investment activity, in a country that imports would fall still more".   Conversely with a rise in export opportunities.   If the rise in exports had a strongly stimulating effect on domestic investment, its net effect might be a deterioration in the country's balance of trade.

How are we to relate this situation to the fourfold doctrine for curative measures set out in the first section of this chapter? No short answer can be given to this question.   It has been the purpose of this handbook to explain the traditional theory of foreign trade, duly modified to take account of the thought of Keynes and his school; even when so modified, this doctrine relates to what has been called a static equilibrium, whether of the short or the long period.   But as soon as we touch on the possible reaction of the level of investment to the increase

---

[1] Let ΔE stand for the increase in the value of exports after the change; this may be positive or negative.   Let i' be the propensity to import in the new situation (which is less than i) and Y^o the level of income prior to the change.   If the change has a net favourable effect on the balance, prior to considering its multiplier effect, then

$$\Delta E - (i' - i)Y^o > O.$$

Let us call the value of this expression B.   This will have a multiplier effect on income, as follows:

$$\Delta Y = B\left(\frac{1}{s+i'}\right).$$

This increase of income will increase imports by the following amount:

$$i'\Delta Y = B\left(\frac{i'}{s+i'}\right).$$

The improvement in the balance prior to the multiplier effect is B, and the deterioration in the balance due to the multiplier effect is $B\left(\dfrac{i'}{s+i'}\right)$, which is evidently less than the improvement.

in some factor of demand (whether on export account or other), we must enter the terrain of dynamic theory. Until quite recently this was allowed to rust; the recent pioneering work of a number of writers has not yet provided a well-developed theory. Accordingly we have to confine ourselves here to certain hints about the right lines of thinking.

In dynamics the concept corresponding to the stable equilibrium of statics is a steady rate of growth. In statics the symptoms of a substantial displacement of aggregate demand from its equilibrium level may be fairly evident—inflationary symptoms or unemployment. The assessment of dynamic equilibrium may require more judgment, including a forward extrapolation of trends. A particular rate of growth may seem very high by past experience, yet fundamental conditions may have so changed as to allow a much higher steady rate of growth than had prevailed before. (Static theory also has to cope with changes in fundamental conditions.)

Proceeding from the particular to the general, we may take the third case specified in § 1 leading to the discussion in § 2, where there is initially unemployment and an adverse balance. It is required to raise exports (E) and to diminish the propensity to import (i) by a sufficient amount, (a) to correct the prevailing adverse balance, and (b) to offset the further deterioration in the balance which will be caused by raising the prevailing low level of income (Y) to a higher level, so that the new income is equal to the supply potential ($Y + \Delta Y = Y^s$). The net effect of measures tending to improve the external balance must be sufficient to offset the decline in the balance associated with the increase of income (Y) and therefore of imports (iY). We suppose the measures to cause an increase of exports (E) and a decline in the propensity to import (i); both these changes will put an additional strain on domestic productive capacity, namely to meet an enlarged export demand and the new home demand resulting from the switch from imports (decline in i) even although aggregate imports (iY) are rising. This additional load upon domestic capacity may require so much investment in new capacity as to set up inflationary pressure.

This effect of the upsurge of activity in creating a new demand for investment is known as the "accelerator" effect, and has nothing at all to do with the multiplier effect discussed in the last section and in Ch. VI.

To abbreviate our wording, let us suppose that the whole effect of the curative measures is to increase exports (by ΔE), and that the effect on the propensity to import (i) is nil. (For the following analysis a decrease in i may be taken to have the same effect on the economy as a whole as an increase in E.) Let the measures be such as to raise exports to a level $(E+\Delta E)$ at which external trade is balanced with full employment at home. It is clearly desirable to work exports up to this level. But to do so may impose so large a domestic requirement for additional capacity (ΔK) as to cause inflationary pressure.

There are alternative lines of action, the right choice among which may depend on the particular circumstances of the case. The fact that no one solution can be unequivocally prescribed is what gives rise to the view that a certain amount of "planning" is needed to maintain economic equilibrium; planning in this general sense has nothing to do with detailed interferences or controls affecting particular lines of production. We may consider the alternatives in turn.

1. It may be decided to take the necessary measures (e.g. devaluation) to step up exports by the required amount (ΔE) and to tolerate a period of inflationary pressure. The disadvantage of this is that the inflation will, by its effects on prices and delivery delays, itself have an adverse effect on the external balance, thus partly annulling the beneficial effect of devaluation. If the curative effect of devaluation is greatly stressed, this situation may prompt a devaluation which will prove to be excessive after the inflationary period is over. Much will depend also on whether the inflationary pressure is likely to set up an inflationary spiral of wages and prices. Generally inflationary pressure should be tolerated only if it is likely to be small and short-lived.

2. Measures may be taken temporarily to curb domestic consumption—by budget surplus, purchase taxes, hire pur-

chase restrictions, etc.—so that the extra capacity required for exports (ΔE) is partly offset by a diminution in the capacity required to meet home demand (ΔH being negative), and the net amount of extra investment needed is reduced to a level that does not cause inflationary pressure. If consumption is reduced this may also release productive resources to expedite the increase of investment that is required.

3. Not all investment is undertaken for the specific purpose of supplying capacity immediately required to produce exports or consumer goods. There may be items that are related to long-range improvements, planned, for instance, in the basic industries. It might be desirable to curb investment in this field, in order to make way for the temporary spurt in the investment required to make capacity for producing the extra flow of exports (ΔE).

Alternative 2 seems more Spartan, and therefore more praiseworthy, than alternative 3; but it cannot be unconditionally recommended for this reason, without regard to the circumstances. When we come to dynamic theory, it is no longer possible to keep the eye fixed only on conditions immediately present; it is necessary to take a look forward.

If, prior to the corrective measures, investment is judged, in relation to long-period probabilities, to be running at a rather low level, alternative 2 should be adopted, in order as speedily as possible to raise investment to a higher level, which it is hoped to sustain thereafter. But if this condition is not fulfilled, and the total amount of investment required both to create capacity for the extra exports (ΔE) and for other purposes is excessive in relation to long-run probabilities, involving a once-over hump in the total demand coming to the industries making investment goods, then alternative 3 may be preferable. It may be undesirable to attract too many fluid resources (e.g. labour) into the investment goods industries, if they will not long be required there; more dangerous is the possibility that excessive capacity will be produced for the investment goods industries themselves, which will later become redundant.

4. There is yet another alternative. It could be decided not

to raise exports at once by the full amount required to balance trade in a region of full employment, but to raise them more gradually (e.g. by successive small devaluations). One could then avoid putting an undue strain at any one time on the investment goods industries. This alternative means allowing an adverse balance to continue, although in progressively diminishing amount, for the time being; accordingly it can be adopted only if the country has sufficient reserves of gold (or equivalent) to tide it over the period of deficit. It will need a particularly strong reserve, as the period of successive devaluations will be a time of heavy speculation against its currency. Subject to the availability of the reserve, it may often be the best of the alternatives. However, in the case where foreign trade is largely in goods subject to imperfect competition, one might get the desired result by a once-over devaluation of *moderate* amount, since the improvement in the balance caused by it is likely to accrue fairly slowly.

All these alternatives presuppose that one starts from a disequilibrium of substantial size. The final object of planning would be to prevent any of the disequilibria discussed in this chapter from reaching large dimensions. This would mean watching the rates of growth in the various categories of demand, framing estimates (to be revised, however, at frequent intervals) of the rates likely to be sustainable, and applying such measures as have been discussed, in order to prevent too large a divergence of the actual rate of growth in each particular category from its most probable steady trend.

§ 4. **Growth of Foreign Trade: Some General Considerations.** The simplest case for consideration is where growth at home is at the same rate as abroad and affects the main categories of goods uniformly. The home country's export opportunities would grow at the same rate as her national income and therefore at the same rate as her imports, her propensity to import being assumed unchanged.

If we retain the assumption of uniformity of rates of growth, as between the categories of goods, but suppose unequal rates of growth of national income as between the home country and the rest of the world (owing, for instance, to different rates of growth of population), then it seems advantageous for the home country to have a smaller rate of growth; in that case the tendency will be for the world price level of the home country's exports to rise against the world price level of her imports.

When we advance beyond these simple cases, attention should be concentrated upon the law of comparative costs. One has to consider how growth in the quantity of various factors of production affects the comparative cost relationship. In the analysis of what commonly gives rise to comparative cost differences the main stress has been placed in this hand-book on natural resources—mineral deposits, land of special qualities, etc.—and on the various kinds of know-how. These latter should be taken in the widest sense, to include not only scientific and technological knowledge and skilled crafts-manship, but also capacity for co-operating in large-scale undertakings, for managing labour and for being managed, and, most important of all—because it gives an advantage in forms of production and trade involving complex relationships —honesty, including incorruptibility. It is curious that, while the cardinal importance of honesty was emphasized in the writings on which modern civilization was based, and is a most familiar fact to all who work on the rock face of devel-opment projects, it does not appear to figure largely in modern treatises on international trade theory.

Recent work has tended to stress the unequal endowment of capital from country to country. While this is of the first importance in creating unequal standards of living as between the countries concerned, I have the impression that it does not by itself give rise to substantial differences in *comparative* costs.

We may think of growth as increases in all the various forms of know-how in the different regions. Of first importance is the question whether these increases tend to make the insulated comparative cost structures of the regions, say of the home country and the rest of the world, more similar or less similar

12

than they were before. It does not seem that anything can be said about the probabilities of the case *a priori*. Some writers have tended to assume that the world is becoming more similar; this may be an optical illusion due to perceiving that a particular know-how, which had previously been abundant in region A but rare elsewhere, was becoming abundant everywhere. But this would only necessarily tend to make the world more similar, if A herself was static. If the developments proceeding in A are no less important than those elsewhere, it remains an open question whether the joint effect of progress in A and outside is to produce greater similarity of comparative costs or not.

If the home country and the rest of the world are indeed becoming more similar, the gains accruing to both from trade will be a declining proportion of their joint national incomes. It does not follow that the gains will decline absolutely. The growth of the two regions increases the gains from foreign trade, assuming comparative costs constant, while the supposed change in comparative costs—towards greater similarity—reduces the gains; it is an open question whether the factor of gain will exceed that of loss. If growth makes the insulated comparative cost structures less similar than they were before, the gain due to trade is likely to increase both absolutely and also as a proportion of the national incomes of the regions.

Each of these two cases subdivides into two. Where the comparative cost structure is becoming *less* similar, that may be (i) because the specific factors required to produce the goods that the home country was previously importing increase abroad at a greater rate than at home, or (ii) because the specific factors required to produce the goods that the home country was previously exporting increase at home at a greater rate than abroad. In both cases the volume of trade is likely to increase and the home country (as well as the rest of the world) will gain thereby. In the former case the terms of trade are likely to move in favour of the home country and in the latter case against her. The loss due to the deterioration in the terms of trade, however, is not measured by the change in the terms. The drop in the price at which the home country offers her exports has two components,[1] namely the lower *prices* of the specific factors required to produce them owing to their greater abundance and the lower *quantities* of the non-specific factors required to produce them. The reduction in the export prices due to the latter cause does not represent any loss of advantage to the country; this is sometimes expressed by saying that the "factorial" terms of trade decline less than the commodity terms.

Where the comparative cost structure is becoming more similar, that may be (i) because the specific factors required to produce the goods that the home country was previously exporting increase abroad at a greater rate than at home, or (ii) because the specific factors required to produce the goods that the home country was previously importing increase at home at a greater rate than abroad. In the former case the terms of trade are likely to move against the home country;[2] in the latter case they are likely to move in her favour. It should be remembered that even in the worst case for the home country ((i) of this paragraph), there may be an increase in the absolute gain from trade for the home country. And it should further be remembered that, even where the gain from trade is declining, the national income may none the less be growing.

§ 5. **Summary.** While an imbalance between exports and imports is necessarily linked to an imbalance between domestic saving and investment, these imbalances may be present when there is no imbalance between the aggregate demand and the supply potential in the country, and may be absent where there is an imbalance between aggregate demand and supply

[1] Cf. ch. II, § 5.
[2] This is the case spotlit by Professor J. R. Hicks in his celebrated lecture entitled *The Long-Run Dollar Problem* (*Oxford Economic Papers*, June 1953), where he refers to import-biased inventions. His "non-dollar world" corresponds to the "home country" in our text and his "dollar world" to the "rest of the world".

potential.   The appropriate remedy for one kind of imbalance cannot be assessed without reference to the state of the other kind of balance.

2. The four possible combinations of these two kinds of imbalance have been considered, and it has appeared that appropriate to each are four remedies which may be roughly designated by the words, reflation, disinflation, devaluation and upward valuation (or upward revision of factor rewards).

3. The success of devaluation is, however, subject to certain limitations; it depends on elasticities of supply and demand being sufficient; it seems likely that in most cases they would be so, at least in the long run.   But it is dangerous to assume that they would be so, without careful study, when the initial maladjustment that has to be corrected is very large.

4. If the remedy has a corrective effect prior to taking its multiplier effect into account, it will do so, albeit to a less extent, after taking that effect into account.

5. It cannot be relied on to do so, however, after taking its accelerator effect into account, if it has one.   This matter can only be analysed in the light of a complete theory of dynamic economics, which is unhappily still in a rudimentary condition. When the effect of an increase in a factor of demand (exports, home consumption, etc.) on the volume of investment has to be taken into account, it is not likely that the rules for action can be so simply formulated.   The policy (sometimes called "planning") required of the central economic authority will become more complex.

6. In the development of a dynamic foreign trade theory the analysis should be focused on movements in the comparative cost differences between countries, whether towards greater or towards less similarity.

CHAPTER VIII

A REFORMED WORLD

§ **1. Good Neighbourliness.** In the last chapter criteria for action by a country were formulated with sole reference to the economy of that country. The maxims there set out may have to be modified, if we take a wider view and give weight to the principle of good neighbourliness. Boom and depression are often world wide phenomena; it may be right for a country to frame its own policy by reference to its membership of the world community.

In regard to the first two cases examined, no sharp conflict appears to arise. In the first case a country was considered which had unemployment at home and a favourable external balance, and the recipe recommended was internal expansion; an illustration was given from the United States in the 'thirties. The policy of expansion would not only have been correct from the self-interested point of view of the United States, but would have been of general benefit; rising imports (iY) by the United States, consequent upon an expansion of her income (Y), would have transmitted to the outside world a welcome force making for recovery. In the second case (internal inflation and external deficit) the remedy of deflation would appear to be salutary. If the world generally is in a phase of boom, the recipe of deflation would appear to be beneficial not only to the country concerned, but to the world economy considered as a unity.

In the third case, however, there is a conflict. This is the case of internal depression and external deficit. From the point of view of the country itself, the recipe laid down was to procure an expansion of exports (E) and a reduction in the propensity to import (i), for example by some such method as devaluation. But if the whole world is suffering from acute depression, such a policy would conflict with the maxim of good neighbourliness. The attempt to capture foreign markets by offering goods at lower prices would increase the *foreign* propensity to import (i), and the attempt by the country to decrease its own propensity to import (i) would decrease the exports (E) of the rest of the world. Both these processes would have a depressive tendency on the rest of the world, which we suppose by hypothesis to be already suffering from depression. It may happen that the home country, being faced with an adverse balance, has no choice but to set up this depressive influence. It would be more desirable from the world point of view if it were able to tolerate its own adverse balance for the time being, and even to aggravate it by promoting measures increasing activity at home, drawing meanwhile upon its reserves. Devaluation, aggravated perhaps by import restrictions, is not to be recommended from the world point of view for any country during a world depression. If the country in question is suffering from "fundamental disequilibrium", so that even after a world recovery from the slump its balance remains adverse, then in the end devaluation may be desirable for that country; but from the world point of view it would be better for this remedy to be postponed until after the worst of the world depression was over.

Such a policy on the part of a country so circumstanced would be a bold one, and the country can hardly be expected to adopt it, unless fortified by some measure of mutual agreement among countries that this is the right policy for deficit countries during world slumps, and perhaps by some international provision for facilitating such policies. Thought on these lines was expressed in the 1939 edition of this handbook.

"The policy of good neighbourliness would be easier of fulfilment if mutual international credits could be granted liberally. In a world recession, all countries should do their utmost to stimulate capital outlay. Countries with a strong passive balance can only do so by depleting their reserves or allowing their exchange rates to run down to an alarming extent. It cannot be denied that however indoctrinated with anti-cycle principles they may be—and such indoctrination is still a thing of the future [1]—there will be a strong psychological resistance to pushing the policy *à l'outrance*. If the liberal granting of international credit could come to be recognized as a normal procedure in depressions, this psychological inhibition might be reduced.

Tariffs, quotas, and import restrictions of all sorts have not so far been discussed, belonging as they do to the pathology of the subject. It cannot be gainsaid that, in a depression, the universal decline of exports and the accentuation of passive balances in some countries set up a strong temptation to use this particular form of un-neighbourly remedy. A routine provision of foreign credit in the depression should reduce the strength of the second of these inducements.

This scheme need not be supposed to demand any self-sacrifice from the creditor countries. These credits would not be granted to particular traders but to the central banks (or exchange funds) of other countries. Moreover some such institution as the Bank for International Settlements might arrange by arbitrage operations that each particular creditor country should have a well distributed assortment of foreign holdings, so that no creditor need be too much concerned with the stability of any particular foreign country. It cannot be regarded as a self-sacrifice to have a lot of foreign money in your possession, provided that there is no reasonable danger of the value of the money depreciating. And, if the creditor countries were uneasy, they would have the remedy in their own hands. They have only to stimulate employment within their own area and thereby imports, to bring their own active balance to an end and thereby liquidate their holdings. It is the very special duty of countries with an active balance in a depression, to bring

[1] But since 1939 to some extent achieved.

it to an end at the earliest possible date by measures of internal expansion."

Such ideas were in the minds of many during the war, and had influence on those who were engaged in discussing post-war reconstruction and were responsible for the setting up of the International Monetary Fund.

The fourth situation also gives rise to a conflict in principle. In this case the country having internal inflationary pressure and a favourable external balance is recommended to redress the latter by some such method as an upward valuation of its currency. It must be observed, however, that the consequent fall in its exports (E) and increase in its propensity to import (i) will tend to increase the inflationary pressures existing outside. It is of course incumbent on the other countries to adopt their own measures for reducing their inflationary pressures. None the less, it cannot be denied that action of the kind prescribed for the country (or countries) with a favourable balance will intensify the problems of the rest.

This was the situation existing in the United States for periods after the war. It certainly helped other countries in a notable degree that the United States did not immediately insist on having an equal external balance, but was willing to cover her favourable balance by the extension of aid for a period. The noble and generous project of Marshall Aid did indeed have wider objects. But one of its purposes, quite correctly conceived, was to make it easier for other countries to get the better of their inflationary difficulties.

The de-valuation of sterling and of other currencies may be regarded as amounting to an upward valuation of the dollar, which was the correct recipe for the United States from the point of view considered in the last chapter, but not from that of the world as a whole. This puts the case against the 1949 devaluations already set forth in the setting of wider principles. It would have been better to have waited until the other countries had brought their de-flationary policies to fruition and to have judged whether a "fundamental disequilibrium" existed or not after these deflationary measures had had their effect. The de-valuation exacerbated the inflationary tendencies in all the countries affected and made their fight against inflation much more difficult.

In normal times one would have to envisage the provision of means for allowing certain countries to remain for a period in deficit, in the form of credit rather than of aid. Credits on the scale of Marshall Aid are hardly to be envisaged. But in normal times the maladjustments in the external balances of countries, even during depressions, are not likely to be nearly so great as those which occurred as an aftermath of the Second World War.

§ 2. **International Monetary Fund.** During the war, the British Authorities put forward a plan for a "Clearing Union", of which Lord Keynes was the principal author, while the Americans put forward a stabilization fund, of which Harry White was the principal author. It may be well first to enumerate four of the leading ideas which were in the mind of the former.

(i) It was desirable greatly to increase the amount of liquid reserves available to various countries. This would enable them to carry forward during depressions without adopting any of the recipes to which they would otherwise be driven, namely (a) deflation, which would be bad for themselves and unneighbourly, (b) devaluation, which would be unneighbourly, or (c) import restrictions, which would be unneighbourly. Both de-valuation and restriction are likely to set up a vicious circle of de-valuations and restrictions which, while helping each country temporarily, would make the situation worse for all.

(ii) In the foregoing analysis attention has been paid to measures appropriate to redress an imbalance whether on the credit or debit side. It has to be observed, however, that, when a nation is in debit, it is under pressure to take action to redress the situation, while a nation in credit may allow its imbalance to continue, merely letting its reserves run up. It has been suggested above that a mere inflow of gold is not

13

likely automatically to secure the cessation of a favourable balance, if reinforcing measures are not taken. But a credit nation may not be under the necessity to take such measures, and indeed may have good reasons for not doing so. Yet if corrective measures are not taken by the credit partners to an imbalance, this may make the position more difficult for the debit partners. Keynes' idea was to establish an international mechanism that would secure an equal sharing between the two kinds of partners of the responsibility for correcting an imbalance.

(iii) The foregoing analysis has suggested that there are situations in which the appropriate remedy for a country in imbalance is de-valuation. This takes account of the practical difficulties and probable inequity of securing the same result by an outright reduction of monetary rewards to factors. After Britain's departure from the gold standard in 1931, there was for some years no fixed par between sterling and the dollar, although the operations of the Exchange Equalization Account (see Chapter V, § 6 above) had much reduced the fluctuations that would otherwise have occurred. Large fluctuations are inimical to the flow of trade and investment; Keynes' idea was to combine the advantages of steady exchanges with a recognition that a change in the rate of exchange was an appropriate remedy for imbalance in certain circumstances.

(iv) Keynes had the idea that it would be desirable to establish a world central bank, which could expand or contract credit on a world-wide scale, rather as each central bank does for each particular country. Operations of this sort were not specifically provided for in his plan, but it was of a kind that would allow them and certain hints were given.

I shall deal with these points in turn.

(i) The Americans were less impressed with the need for a very large increase of liquid reserves. They had not themselves had practical experience of the awkwardness arising from a shortage of reserves for more than thirty years. Keynes' plan would have resulted in the provision of mutual credits as between nations on a very large scale. The Americans feared that in practice the mutuality would have been somewhat one-sided, and have amounted to a large scale "hand-out" by themselves; post-war events suggest that their fears might have been justified by the event. None the less the question of principle remained.

The International Monetary Fund embodies provisions for mutual credit, but on a much smaller scale than that proposed by Keynes. Meanwhile a situation has arisen which does not appear to have been foreseen in the discussions about these matters. Owing to the great inflation of prices, including dollar prices, during and after the war, which has since been consolidated, the commodity value of gold has been reduced to less than half its pre-war value. Both existing stocks and the annual output of gold have now a greatly reduced commodity value; consequently the liquid reserves available for countries are much reduced, in relation to the requirements of world trade, even if we reckon in the drawing rights on the International Monetary Fund of the various countries. In regard to the possibility of countries refraining from un-neighbourly action during depressions on the lines suggested in paragraph (i) above, the position, so far from having improved, is very much worse than it was before the war. This is probably the principal reason why countries have been quicker to resort to the unneighbourly remedy of import restriction during recent years.

(ii) Keynes proposed to cast an equal share of responsibility for correcting an imbalance on to credit countries by providing that they should accumulate their favourable balances in the form of Bancor (the currency of the Clearing Union), in order that they should have a strong motive for taking corrective measures to obviate an excessive piling up of Bancor in their name. The American negotiators deemed that this remedy would be unacceptable to the American Congress. To meet the point that a credit country should share responsibility, they offered instead the "scarce currency clause", which has been incorporated in the Articles of Agreement of the International Monetary Fund. This provides a different kind of remedy. It has already been explained why it is undesirable for nations in deficit to impose import restrictions during a depression; one reason is that it will lead to a vicious circle of restrictions. But if one nation (or more) shows a persistently credit balance, the imposition of restrictions on imports from such nation or nations only will not set up a vicious circle, since those nations being, by hypothesis, in a credit position will not need to impose restrictions in their turn. The general philosophy of the planning for the post-war world comprised the view that discrimination in commercial or monetary arrangements was undesirable. The scarce currency clause is in effect an admission of an exception to this general principle. If various nations are in deficit, it is better that they should confine any restrictions that they have to impose on their imports to imports from nations whose own external balances are favourable. This is a form of discrimination; it is economically desirable because it confines the incidence of restriction to those nations not likely, by hypothesis, to pass the restriction on. It allows nations to employ restrictions, which it may be essential for them to do in the circumstances, but encourages them to confine their restrictions to goods coming from the persistently credit countries.

Although the dollar has been scarce during periods since the war, the International Monetary Fund has thought it the wiser course not to allow such drawings upon it as would compel them to declare the dollar a "scarce" currency. It would indeed have been inexpedient and churlish to have declared the dollar scarce in a period when the Americans were taking such very generous action in covering the dollar deficit of the rest of the world with them by various forms of aid.

Whether the scarce currency clause will ever come into action as a normal method for adjusting an international imbalance remains to be seen. It has one objectionable feature, which was inserted at a late stage of drafting. If one nation is in persistent credit balance, and if the only available remedy is thought to be a restriction by other nations of their imports from the credit nation, it would be desirable that all nations should impose restrictions more or less equi-proportionately. The clause, however, only allows nations which are specifically short of dollars to impose such restric-tions; this piece of "bilateralist" thinking accords ill with the philosophy of multilateral trade and settlement on which the International Monetary Fund is in other respects based. It is also doubtful if this provision would have any meaning, if the currencies of members of the Fund were all convertible, as envisaged by the Articles of Agreement.

(iii) The proposal to combine short-run stability with the right of members to re-value their currencies in the event of "fundamental disequilibrium" has been adopted. The Fund was set up after the war, most nations of the world joined it, and, when doing so, recorded the parities at which they would be willing to hold their currencies, subject to the right to re-value later in the event of a fundamental disequilibrium. It can surely not be doubted that the fact that various nations established parities for their currencies has been an important check upon currency disorders and inflations, such as occurred after the first world war. Had the Fund not existed or had nations not thought it worthwhile to join and to comply with its provisions in some measure, there would surely have been much more extensive currency depreciation and other forms of disorder.

The recognition that an orderly devaluation may be appro-priate is also a gain. The fact that the devaluations of 1949, undertaken in conditions of extreme post-war pressure, were ill starred, need not be taken as a serious ill augury for the satisfactory working of this provision in future.

Some doubt must be raised, however, upon whether the combination of a fixed par with occasional devaluation will function so smoothly as a means of combining short-run stability with long-run flexibility, as did the arrangements of the British Exchange Equalization Account (see Chapter V, § 6 above). The former, unlike the latter, is apt to provoke undesirable speculation, which may in turn make it difficult to determine whether the currency of a particular country is in fundamental disequilibrium or not. In Keynes' original plan each country was entitled to allow the value of its currency to alter by not more than 5% in any one year on its own initiative. A change in value of more than this would have required the sanction of the Fund, but would only have been likely to be required in very rare and exceptional circumstances. It may be that this would be a better method for combining short-run steadiness with long-run flexibility than that provided by the Fund.

(iv) The structure of the Clearing Union would have allowed it to operate, if required, like a world central bank in creating monetary ease or restriction in the world as a whole from time to time. The structure of the Fund was based on the American proposal for a Stabilization Fund; its resources consist of a bag full of world currencies supplied at the outset, and it has accordingly not the power to expand or contract the supply of money on a world scale.

The establishment of the Fund has been an important advance along the road of international monetary co-operation. Much more will, however, be needed if the principles for correcting the two kinds of imbalance, as outlined in Chapter VII and modified in the interests of good neighbourliness in § 1 of this chapter, are to be carried out by the different nations acting in co-operation.

§ 3. International Bank for Reconstruction and Development.
The purpose of this Bank, which was planned at the same time as the International Monetary Fund, is to revive the flow of international investment. The importance of this has been indicated at a number of places. The Bank is likely to direct its main attention to investment in under-developed countries, mobilizing for the purpose the savings of those more advanced. A special agency was required for this, because private international investment has declined owing both to economic and to political shocks to confidence. The Bank made a very good

start in its first ten years. It should make contributions of increasing amount in its highly important task.

The investments promoted by it should not be expected to have a corrective effect on the world imbalance of payments. Its aim will be to raise money in the several countries in proportion to the demand upon each for capital goods arising from the sponsored projects. To the extent that this aim is realized, extra exports by the countries supplying capital goods will be exactly matched by their extra foreign lending. In its early days it made a slight (temporary) contribution to correcting the world dollar imbalance by providing slightly more dollars than were required for the investment projects that it sponsored; this will only have been a temporary easement because loans made in dollars, or in foreign currencies acquired by it by the sale of its own dollars, are repayable to it in dollars.

§ 4. G.A.T.T. At the time of the discussions for post-war currency and banking arrangements, it was hoped to secure a reduction of tariffs and other trade barriers on a world wide multilateral basis, and to set up an Institution (International Trade Organization) for continually promoting this object. This plan did not mature in its original form, but instead a General Agreement on Trade and Tariffs has led to successive conferences for this purpose. Although far reaching reductions, such as were originally hoped for, have not been secured, some useful work has been done in getting moderate reductions, and much credit must be given to these meetings for preventing large increases in trade barriers, such as might otherwise have occurred.

§ 5. E.P.U. The large maladjustments in the balance of trade, which were due to the war and its aftermath, led to world wide restrictions on the negotiability of currencies (as described in Chapter V, § 8 above), and these tended to force trade into a bilateral pattern. Each country had to give thought to its external balance of payments, not only with the world as a whole, but also with each other country considered

separately.   The extension of Marshall Aid to the countries of
Europe gave an impetus and opportunity for plans for re-
introducing multilateralism within the western European
region.   It seemed desirable for a region to go ahead of the
re-establishment of full multilateralism on a world wide basis,
because the world dollar imbalance was still an obstacle to
the latter.   (British membership brought with it that of the
whole sterling area.)

For this purpose "E.P.U. Units of Account" were invented
(not unlike the Bancor in Keynes' Clearing Union scheme),
and the net credit or debit positions of participating countries
inside Europe were expressed in these units, so that each
country ceased to be worried about its balance of payments
position with each other European country considered separately, and only had to concern itself with its balance with the
rest of Europe as a whole.   This was reinforced by commitments by the participating countries to provide mutual credits
in respect of a portion of the net debit position arising at the
end of each month.   This currency plan was associated with
commitments to reduce quantitative restrictions on imports
from other European countries ("liberalization").   The
combined effect of these measures was to increase the flow of
intra-European trade.

After the war the countries of Western Europe were
especially severely affected by the problem of trade imbalance.
This continued even after the productive capacity of these
countries was restored to the pre-war level and raised above it.
In relation to the dollar balance, the most important reason
for the changed position was the greatly reduced value of the
annual output of new gold, which Europe had before the war
bought from its surpluses outside the dollar area and used to
settle its normal deficits with the dollar area (see page 173
above).   The large gap left by the reduction in the value of
this acceptable mode of settling with the United States proved
difficult to fill by other commodities for the United States
market.   The trade barriers of the United States, although
reduced, remained a serious obstacle, which was increased

by uncertainties in regard to future U.S. tariffs. Uncertainties about future tariffs are often as great an obstacle to trade as the tariffs themselves. On the side of European trade with the rest of the world, her balance had been severely hit (i) by a large deterioration in the "terms of trade", and (ii) by the loss of "invisible" income from overseas investments, many of which had been realized during the war. Thus not only was there a direct dollar problem, but also an initial difficulty in re-establishing a balance with the outside world as a whole. The latter problem did not prove too difficult to solve, but the former remained obdurate.

The multilateralism established inside Europe by the E.P.U. and allied undertakings may thus be considered as a half-way house. It has been argued that this partial multilateralism might discourage efforts to re-establish equilibrium in the wider sphere. The mutual credits referred to tended to make European currencies "soft" *vis-à-vis* each other by comparison with the currencies of the outside world. The authorities tend to encourage imports from soft currency areas and to discourage exports to them. But as the authorities can have a greater effect in influencing the provenance of imports than the destination of exports, it has been argued that the net effect of the mutual softening of European currencies would be to divert European exports from outside countries to markets inside Europe. The validity of this view depends on the phase of the trade cycle. When there is slackness in the economy, the increased demand for exports coming from other European countries should have no injurious effect on European exports to the outside world. But when there is inflationary pressure and export customers have to be put on a waiting list, then the argument quoted may have some validity.

Some hold that with the restoration of the convertibility of currencies on a multilateral world wide basis, the European Payment Union will quietly fade away. The other view is that it can still play a useful part; there is a proposal that a "European Fund" should be created; the net effect of the E.P.U. arrangement has been to increase liquidity, by the mutual credits provided; as the most acute problem of all in international economics has been the great shortage of liquidity since the war, it would be a pity to dispense with any net contribution, albeit one on a regional basis, to the amount of international liquidity available.

§ **6. Summary.** It appears that the move since the war towards greater international co-operation has been piecemeal and not very extensive. It is thought, however, that the next step should be for all the nations to get their own houses more thoroughly in order. The thinking that has taken place and the plans that have been made, incomplete and fragmentary as these have been, make it quite certain that, should a world wide depression recur, there would be quick moves towards closer collaboration between the various countries. If no depression occurs, but a phase of high activity, tending towards inflationary pressure, continues, the main emphasis will be on the separate actions of national Governments. At the same time we may hope for moderate improvements and refinements in the machinery for co-operation.

APPENDIX

THE principles by which the figures in the tables in Chapter II are calculated may be explained as follows:

1. Tables VII, IX and XI. It is assumed that cost gradients are in all four cases linear and proportional to initial costs in the respective countries. Transport costs are neglected.

Let r be the final ratio of the cost of wheat to the cost of coal, at home and abroad, as it is established in the final equilibrium. $1/r$ thus represents the number of units of wheat that can be had in exchange for one unit of coal in that equilibrium. Let q be the change in cost consequent on the shift in production due to the opening of trade. Let p be the initial cost abroad of 1 unit of coal prior to the opening of trade. (Other initial costs are each 1 by the definition of the units of product and cost.)

The final position may be represented as follows:

	Cost at home	Cost abroad
Unit of wheat	$1-q$	$1+q$
Unit of coal	$1+q$	$p(1-q)$

We then have:

$$\frac{1-q}{1+q}=r=\frac{1+q}{p(1-q)}$$

from which it follows that:

$$r=\frac{1}{\sqrt{p}} \quad \dots (1)$$

and

$$q=\frac{1-r}{1+r} \quad \dots (2)$$

These equations suffice for the calculation of the final positions on various assumptions as to the value of p, i.e. the degree of initial disparity of cost ratios.

In the first edition of this book the cost of a unit of wheat in final equilibrium was written down as $1 - \frac{q}{r}$ at home and $1 + \frac{q}{r}$ abroad, on the ground that the reduction in the number of units of wheat produced at home would be greater, in the proportion $\frac{1}{r}$, than the increase in the number of units of coal, since $\frac{1}{r}$ units of wheat could be obtained in foreign trade per unit of coal exported. The insertion of $\frac{1}{r}$ in the upper lines of all the tables necessarily complicated the calculations and, on reflection, I have decided that it is inappropriate. (It also leads to somewhat unrealistic conclusions.) The question turns on what units of coal and wheat we use when we work on the assumption that their cost gradients are proportional to initial costs. In the first edition I adhered to the units of product contained in the initial definitions (viz. one unit of coal is that amount of coal which costs the same to produce as one unit of wheat, before trade, in the home country). But these units have no special validity. It must be remembered that the facts set out in Table V in the text could be equally well represented as follows, by merely defining a unit of coal as that amount of coal which cost the same to produce in the outside world, before trade, as a unit of wheat:

INITIAL POSITION

			Cost at home	Cost abroad
Unit of wheat	.	.	.	$1x$	$1y$
Unit of coal	.	.	.	$\frac{1}{4}x$	$1y$

Taking these units, r in the final equilibrium would be not 1:2, but 2:1. By this definition a unit of coal would only be one-quarter of the unit of coal as defined for the purpose of Table V. As conditions at home have no logical priority over those abroad, or vice versa, it has seemed most natural and appropriate to take the geometric mean of these two units, giving a final ratio of 1:1, in calculating the cost gradient. Then, since $r=1$ (*for this purpose only*) it disappears from the top row expressions in Tables VII, IX and XI. More generally it has seemed expedient for the purpose of calculating proportional cost gradients, to take 1 unit of coal to be that amount of coal which exchanges for 1 unit of wheat in the final equilibrium. This enables us to dispense with any reference to r in the top row expressions in all the tables. It seems most natural to take 1 unit of coal to be that amount which exchanges for 1 unit of wheat after the world has entered into full trading relations. It is to be remembered that in postulating proportional gradients, we are not asserting anything as fact or as the most probable relation. We are merely concerned to set up a schema whereby the effect of varying certain variables, including the gradients themselves, may be demonstrated.

2. Table XIII. I have assumed gradients to be in inverse proportion to the amount of production in the region. Let n represent the ratio of home production to the production of the outside world prior to trade. We then have:

FINAL POSITION

	Cost at home	Cost abroad
Unit of wheat . . .	$1-q$	$1+nq$
Unit of coal . . .	$1+q$	$p(1-nq)$

3. Tables XIV and XV. g is the change in cost in the home country per unit change in the amount produced divided by $1/n$ times the change in cost abroad per unit change in the amount produced. We then have:

FINAL POSITION

	Cost at home	Cost abroad
Unit of wheat . . .	$1-gq$	$1+nq$
Unit of coal . . .	$1+gq$	$p(1-nq)$

In Table XV $n=1$

Reference is made in the text (p. 31) to gain per unit of foreign trade. This it is impossible to determine in absolute terms without knowing how much the rise in the cost of producing coal is due to "rent" elements (cf. p. 26). If it were entirely due to rent, then the gain per unit of trade would be equal to the new ratio minus the pre-trade ratio, viz. in Table XV, 1·59.. minus 1. If no rent element entered in, then, assuming equal gradients for wheat and coal, it would be half this. In comparing Table XV with Table IX it is proper to assume that the same proportion of the rise in the cost of coal is due in both cases to rent. Since, for the comparison, it is not needful to know the absolute amount of gain per unit, we may take ·59.. (viz. 1·59−1) as the measure of the gain in Table XV to be compared with ·414.. (viz. 1·414−1) as the measure of the gain in Table IX.

A Tariff and the Quantity and Terms of Trade

Let a uniform tariff of amount t be imposed by the home country, where t stands for the ratio of tariff to price. Represent $(1+t)$ by T

The schema for full trade is as follows:

				Cost at home	Cost abroad
Unit of wheat	.	.	.	$1-gq$	$1+nq$
Unit of coal	.	.	.	$1+gq$	$p(1-nq)$
Ratio of costs	.	.	.	Tr	r

In the case where $g=1$ and $n=1$

$$r=\frac{1}{\sqrt{T}\,\sqrt{p}}$$

and

$$q=\frac{\sqrt{p}-\sqrt{T}}{\sqrt{p}+\sqrt{T}}$$

The terms of trade confronting the home country are represented by r. The smaller is r, the more favourable are the terms. Let r represent the terms under free trade and r_1 the terms when there is a tariff of t_1. In comparing the gain *per unit of trade* when there is a given tariff with the free trade position, we may take $1-r_1$ and $1-r_0$ as indexes of gain per unit. This implies that rent elements play the same proportional part in both cases.

Any tariff increases the gain per unit of trade while reducing the quantity of trade. It seems that in most cases, where the rest of the world is at all large by comparison with the home country, any tariff whatever will reduce the quantity by a greater proportion than it increases the gain per unit, and will thus cause a net loss. This is not in line with some doctrines that have been propounded recently.

I am not able to supply a general formula. The upshot depends primarily (i) on the size of the world in comparison with the home country ($1/_s$ above) and (ii) on the degree of divergence of comparative costs (p above). Where the divergence is large, there is greater scope for the possibility of gain by tariff. If trade is reduced by a tariff to vanishing point, the most favourable value that r can achieve is $1/_p$. Consequently the scope for an improvement in r, as trade is cut off, depends on the amount of its divergence from $1/_p$ in the free trade position. Where the rest of the world is relatively large, this divergence is in any case small; consequently the rate of improvement in the ratio, as trade is reduced, is small and a tariff must bring net loss. But the chance that r will diverge substantially from $1/_p$ in the free trade position is greater, the greater is p.

Where the difference in comparative cost is no more than in the ratio $2:1$ ($p=2$), it appears that a tariff will involve a net loss whenever the rest of the world is somewhat larger than the home country. Where the rest of the world is four times as great as the home country or more, it appears that there will be net loss for all values of p. But where the rest of the world is substantially smaller than this and p is very large, there are possibilities of net gain.

It is to be noted that the measure of gain provided by the

schema is a hard physical measure. It operates in terms of the quantity of wheat that can be secured for a country by the devotion of a given quantity of resources to the production of coal for export instead of devoting them to the direct production of wheat. It does not allow for further gains from trade that may accrue when *demand* is taken into account and new consumers' surpluses accrue through the adaptation of consumer budgets to the new price structure set up in consequence of trade.

MADE AND PRINTED IN GREAT BRITAIN BY WILLIAM CLOWES AND SONS, LIMITED
LONDON AND BECCLES